Books by Helene Hanff

Q'S LEGACY

HELENE HANFF

Q'S

LEGACY

Little, Brown and Company
BOSTON • TORONTO

FIRST EDITION

Library of Congress Cataloging in Publication Data

Hanff, Helene.
  Q's legacy.

  1. Hanff, Helene — Biography. 2. Authors, American —
20th century — Biography. 3. Quiller-Couch, Arthur
Thomas, Sir, 1863–1944 — Influence — Hanff. I. Title.
PS3515.A4853Z473 1985   818'.5409 [B]   85-4268
ISBN 0-316-34340-4

BP

DESIGNED BY DEDE CUMMINGS

*Published simultaneously in Canada
by Little, Brown & Company (Canada) Limited*

PRINTED IN THE UNITED STATES OF AMERICA

In grateful memory of
SIR ARTHUR QUILLER-COUCH

"Not to pay a debt but to acknowledge it."

⋙ CONTENTS ⋘

Q'S LEGACY

⇛ ONE ⇚

How It All Started

Q AND I FIRST MET on a summer morning when I was eighteen, at the main branch of the Philadelphia Public Library where I'd gone in search of a teacher; and I took him home with me despite certain doubts about his fitness for the post.

This was during the Depression, at the end of my only year at college. Knowing my parents couldn't afford to send me to college, I'd gone to a special academic high school that taught its students to compete for college scholarships. In my second year (when I hit Geometry) I knew I wasn't bright enough to win one of them. I excelled in English and I got good grades in History and languages (I tried Latin, Greek and French in successive years). But I barely passed Geometry, Algebra and Chemistry, and if the teacher hadn't liked me I'd have flunked Physics. And college scholarships went to students with a record of "general excellence" in high school.

Still, there was one scholarship to Temple University my teachers thought I could win. Temple was looking for liberal arts students to enroll in an experimental teacher-training program called "The X Group." Since liberal arts were my best subjects, I took the X Group scholarship exam and — in one of my best subjects — failed so spectacularly I stunned the entire Board of Examiners into sending for me afterward out of morbid curiosity. The subject was History.

Our high school History exams had never included maps, so my teacher never knew I couldn't read them. But a friend warned me that the X Group History exam included "a Map question," and I set out to cram for it. Since we'd studied both American and European history, I decided the Map question would probably deal with both continents. I went to the library and brought home two history books, one with a map of Europe, the other with a map of the forty-eight states. Then I sat down to memorize both of them.

Both maps were oblong. Every country on the map of Europe was in a separate color. So was every state in the Union. I started with the map of Europe and after a few evenings of intense concentration I tested myself. Being very nearsighted, I couldn't read print without my glasses, so I took them off and — unable to see the printed names on the map without them — I triumphantly identified the pink blob down in the left-hand corner as Spain, the purple mass up on the right as Russia and so forth. I knew Europe cold.

Memorizing the forty-eight states was much harder. As I settled at a desk for the History exam, I hoped the Map question would deal with the upper layer of the middle states instead of the lower layer.

The History exam was in two parts, each worth 50 points for a perfect score of 100. Part I was a list of questions requiring written answers and when I finished, I knew I'd gotten close to a perfect 50 on it.

Part II was a large folded sheet of white paper, which, when I opened it, turned out to be a map. It was round, it was black-and-white and it included the entire world. There were no printed place names on it. Under the map was a long list of place names in alphabetical order — Abyssinia to Zanzibar. At the top of the map was a single instruction:

"Insert each place name correctly on the map."

Forget the middle states; on that map I couldn't find Europe. But you don't flunk worse for wrong answers than for no answers and I thought if I inserted all the place names somewhere, by luck and the law of averages I might get a few of them right. As far as I know, I didn't. What stunned the Board of Examiners into sending for me was that after scoring a perfect 50 on the first half of the exam, I'd labeled the Pacific Ocean "Africa."

To sum up: I excelled in English. This won me a one-year scholarship to the X Group, where (by postponing Calculus and Physics till some later year) I got top grades. But when the year ended, the Dean told me regretfully my scholarship couldn't be extended for another year. Because of the deepening Depression, all Temple's scholarship money would have to go to senior students who couldn't graduate without it.

This was a great blow to my parents, but a secret relief to me. In my year at Temple I'd learned nothing about English literature or the art of writing, which was all I wanted to learn. In the fall I would be free to find my own teacher.

That June I got a job in a bookshop, substituting for the regular assistant who was going to Maine with her parents for the summer. And when she told me business in the bookshop was very slow in summer and I'd have long empty hours there, I decided my education wouldn't have to wait till fall. I was to start work in the bookshop on a July Monday, and on the Saturday before, I took the subway downtown to the imposing main branch of the library. I went into the vast circulation room and asked the lady behind the desk where I'd find books on English literature, especially college textbooks. She sent me to a double aisle of bookshelves marked 800 and told me which subdivisions to look under.

Standing there, staring at the long shelves crammed with books, I felt myself relax and I was suddenly at peace. I knew who I was and what I was doing there, and I had all day to find what I was looking for.

The books were arranged alphabetically by author and I started with the A's, taking down one volume and then another, reading the author's credentials — "Chairman, English Department, Vassar College"; "Professor of English at Yale University" — and then the chapter headings and the first few paragraphs of a chapter.

I worked my way through the M's without finding what I wanted. What I wanted was the Best — written in language I could understand. I hadn't defined "the Best" but I was discovering what it wasn't. Most of the textbooks confined themselves to nineteenth- and twentieth-century writers, omitting what I'd been taught were the greatest works of English literature: Shakespeare, Milton and the Bible. And all of them were written in learned, academic language that was over my head.

I went on through the N's, O's and P's, fighting a suspicion that what I wanted didn't exist.

There was only one book under Q.

ON THE ART OF WRITING
by
Sir Arthur Quiller-Couch, M.A.
King Edward VII Professor of English Literature
in the University of Cambridge

The dust-jacket biography told me the author was a graduate of Trinity College, Oxford, and that the book was one of several volumes of lectures delivered to his students at Jesus College, Cambridge, where he still taught. It added that he was also the author of popular novels which were signed simply "Q," the nickname by which he was known to his students.

If you wanted instruction in how to read and write English, Oxford-and-Cambridge was definitely the Best. I ran my eye down the list of chapter headings:

"On the Practise of Writing"
"On the Capital Difficulty of Verse"
"On the Capital Difficulty of Prose"

I could understand them.

Chapter V was headed: "Interlude: On Jargon." Since I didn't know what "Jargon" was, I turned to the chapter and began to read, and came to a pair of sentences set off in the middle of the page:

He was conveyed to his place of residence in an intoxicated condition.
He was carried home drunk.

Q said that the first sentence was Jargon and the second was good English prose.

I thought it was a misprint; the printer must have got the two sentences backward. I read a little further and came to a quote from a Prime Minister in the House of Commons:

"The answer to the question is in the negative."

"That means No," said Q. "Can you discover it to mean anything more? — except that the speaker is a pompous person, which was no part of the information required."

So it wasn't a misprint.

I was very shocked. I liked long fancy words; I thought they were literary. I didn't want to write "He was carried home drunk" all my life; it was lower class. But I read a little more and came to a phrase I'd seen in dozens of textbooks as a chapter heading: "Transition Period" — "which means," said Q, "we haven't much to say, just about here."

I stood staring at the page with the two glaringly wrong sentences set off in the middle of it, and considered Q's pros and cons. He spoke a language I could understand, and he had a sense of humour, which all by itself set him apart from the rest of the professors I'd been reading all morning. And he was Oxford-and-Cambridge. I decided I could study with him without necessarily agreeing with everything he said. I took home *On the Art of Writing* and one other book of his lectures.

Both were four-week books and at the end of four weeks I trudged back to the library to renew both of them, in what was turning out to be a very wearing summer. In the first chapter of *On the Art of Writing* he threw so many marvelous quotes at me — from Walton's *Angler*, Newman's *Idea of a University* and Milton's *Paradise Lost* — that I rushed back to the library and brought home all three, determined to read them all before going on to Q's second lecture. Which would have been perfectly possible if I hadn't included *Paradise Lost*. In *Paradise Lost* I ran into Satan, Lucifer, the Infernal Serpent and a Fiend, all of whom seemed to be lurking around the Garden of Eden and none of whom my teachers at Rodeph Shalom Sunday School had ever mentioned to me. I consulted my Confirmation Bible, but I couldn't find Milton's fearsome personages in Genesis. I concluded that Lucifer and the Fiend weren't Jewish and I would have to look in the New Testament for them, and since this was an entirely new book to me, Q had to wait while I read that one, too. But I'd saved enough out of my ten-dollar weekly paycheck by then to buy both books of lectures, freeing me to take my time over them, with plans for taking two more out of the library in the fall.

In September, the bookshop job ended, and when all my friends were going back to college I was happily mapping out a daily course of study with Q: 2 hours of Q, 2 hours of Milton, 2 hours of Shakespeare, 1 hour of English essays (dessert). I began reading industriously all day long, unaware that my Depression-ridden parents were anxiously waiting for me to go out and find another job.

My Uncle Al was living with us at the time. (He'd been my rich Uncle Al till the stock-market crash wiped him out. Now he lived with us as a paying boarder.) My Uncle Al realized that I wasn't trained for the ordinary jobs open to young women. But his former bookkeeper, a Mr. Green, had opened a business school where girls were taught "office skills," and Mr. Green, out of friendship for my uncle, offered to accept me in the school's 90-day secretarial course at a reduced rate. My parents were so grateful for this opportunity I couldn't tell them I wasn't. In November (weeping secretly over it in my room the night before), I had to drop out of Q's classes to study shorthand and typing at Mr. Green's school.

I was a real joy at that business school. Mrs. Green taught our shorthand class and I wasn't there a week before I was obliged to correct her grammar. She dictated a sentence that began: "I cannot help but think" — and I raised my hand and told her the phrase was ungrammatical.

"You can say 'I cannot but think' or you can say 'I cannot help thinking,' " I explained kindly. "But you can't say 'I cannot help but.' It's wrong."

She was a small, worried-looking middle-aged woman with the Depression and us to contend with, and she was too chronically tired to be angry. She just looked confused and mildly resentful and she sent one of the girls for Mr. Smoter to settle the matter. Mr. Smoter taught Business English. He was also young and good-looking and I had a crush on him. Mr. Smoter came and was duly consulted about "I cannot help but think."

"Well, it's not good grammar," he admitted reluctantly, with the eyes of the class glued on him. "It's a double negative."

This coup brought me to the attention of the school leader, an animated black-haired kid named Rita, whose prestige stemmed from the fact that her barber father had once shaved Al Smith, a losing presidential candidate. Rita headed the school's ruling clique and after my triumph over Mrs. Green, she invited me to go along with the clique to the drugstore where they gathered for sodas after school.

Rita and her friends were quick-witted and intelligent; they had no trouble with shorthand or typing, but they spoke a dese-dem-dose English and they sweated to construct simple business letters for Mr. Smoter's class. They were vastly impressed by a classmate who could actually correct a teacher's grammar, and as soon as they learned I hankered after Mr. Smoter, they went to work devising ploys to get him for me. The best was Rita's. She got up in Business English class and suggested that after every Friday's English test, Mr. Smoter award a kiss to whoever got the best score. She made him stick to this award for the rest of the 90 days. Which was one reason why I had such a good time in that school I was almost sorry when the course ended.

Through the next two years and a succession of office jobs, I went on reading Q, and out of my earnings eventually managed to buy all five volumes of his lectures. And broke as we were, when my mother saw a new volume of them displayed in Wanamaker's book department, she bought it for me.

At the beginning of the third year, my Cambridge education hit a snag. As suddenly as if I'd been struck by lightning, I was stagestruck. I joined a Little Theatre group as an actress and I began to write plays in the evening instead of studying with Q. At the end of the Thirties I won a national playwriting contest sponsored by the Theatre Guild. The prize money was to support me for a year while I studied in a seminar for young playwrights to be conducted by the Guild. I moved to New York and my books, and Q, moved with me.

The Theatre Guild was Broadway's most distinguished producing organization, so committed to producing plays for their artistic merit rather than their commercial appeal that Broadway columnists dubbed it "The Thitter Geeld." But the year of the seminar, the Guild's luck seemed to have run out. It produced five straight flops.

Terry Helburn, one of the two Guild producers, made me her protégée, and two years later she gave me a job writing publicity stories in the Guild press department — and the Guild was still producing five flops a year. I loved the job and I loved Terry — five feet tall with fluffy, blue-rinsed white hair and a habit of referring to New York's eight dignified drama critics as "the Boys." ("I don't know what the Boys want," she'd say without rancor, reading the reviews of each successive flop.) I even liked Lawrence Langner, her co-producer, with his neat brown clothes and neat brown mustache and his incessant inter-office memos on Economy. ("Please save the envelope containing this memo. It can be re-used for inter-office memos. We are all wasting too much stationery." "As only three people use the Press Department bathroom, the Empire Linen Rental Service will limit your supply hereafter to three towels per week.")

My job was to write feature stories about the stars of Guild shows, which Joe, the Guild press agent, could place in New York's eight daily newspapers. If the star had a big name (we had Katharine Hepburn in one flop), Joe took her to lunch at Sardi's and I tagged along; he asked the questions and I took stenographic notes of the answers. When the "star" was unknown — like the young ingenue Celeste Holm in another of our flops — I interviewed her by myself in the Press Department over drugstore coffee. But in my third year there, the Theatre Guild astonished Broadway by producing a musical. It was called *Oklahoma!* and it broke the Theatre Guild's losing streak by being a smash hit. This time, when Celeste Holm turned up in the cast, she and I had a high old time over lunch at Sardi's.

The Guild had an unfortunate habit of closing down for three months every June and moving to its summer theatre in Westport, Connecticut, where it got along without most of its New York staff, including me. I had to find my own summer theatre job every June and since it barely paid my summer living expenses, my New York home was a cheap hotel room that I could vacate in June and move back into in September. The room was too small for bookshelves, and anyway I was too broke to buy them. The books I'd brought from home were kept on the closet floor, with the closet shelf reserved for Q.

I'd begun sneaking back into his classes in the evening and guiltily wallowing in Walton and George Herbert and Leigh Hunt when I was supposed to be studying Ibsen, Chekhov and Stanislavski. I got all the books from the public library and — desolately — returned them just as I was learning to love them.

But a year after *Oklahoma!* opened I left the Guild and began to earn a living of sorts working part-time and at home reading, and writing summaries of, plays and novels submitted to the New York Story Department of Paramount Pictures. Since it was steady all-year-round work, I was able to sign a lease on what the English call a "bed-sitter": a furnished living room with a studio couch for sleeping, and the use of a community bath and kitchen up the hall.

It was a big room flooded with sunlight, and I found I could read Paramount's galleys or playscripts in the evening, type my reader's report after breakfast and have the whole day free for writing my bad plays. (They specialized in plotless charm.) I also found that after three years in an office, working at home was like being let out of prison.

In May, a friend gave me her old orange-crate bookshelves and my happiness was complete. I painted them bright blue (to go with the slipcover on my easy chair) and then made a list of the books I wanted to buy.

A few mornings later I was turning the pages of the morning *Times* on my way to the theatre page when I was stopped by a two-column headline above an unfamiliar face, on the Obituary page:

Quiller-Couch, Anthologist
Dies at 80

The obituary writer seemed to regard Q's editing of *The Oxford Book of English Verse* as his principal achievement, and I added it to my book list. Then I sat and studied the controlled, weather-beaten face I'd never seen. I felt suddenly lost with Q gone. Till I looked at the books of his lectures ranged on the top bookshelf and thought: "He's not gone, you nut, you have him in the house!" I cut out the obituary and put it carefully between the pages of *On the Art of Writing*. (It's still there, in dried yellow fragments. I just pieced them together so I could quote the headline for you.)

Then I set out to buy the books he'd taught me to love. Most of them were out of print — or might as well have been. There was one bookshop on Madison Avenue, called Chaucer Head, which displayed gold-embossed, leather-bound classics in the window, and I used to stop and stare at them like a dog at a butcher-shop window. Chaucer Head probably had most of the books I wanted, but the plush interior looked so forbiddingly expensive I never had the nerve to set foot in the place. (If Shakespeare will pardon me, it's poverty does make cowards of us all.) The fine Fifth Avenue bookstores — Brentano's and Scribner's — also had English classics only in fine leather-bound editions I couldn't afford. The modern neighborhood bookstores didn't have them at all. But somebody told me there was a row of secondhand bargain-basement book-stores down on East 17th Street and at the best of them, Barnes & Noble, I found what I wanted. More or less.

Barnes & Noble bought and resold discarded school and college textbooks. In "cloth" bindings. Quotation marks because they felt like cardboard. A few I bought were reasonably clean. Some were horrors. My Catullus, for instance, had an ink-stained cover, and on every page, phrases and paragraphs encircled in decorative graffiti and margins filled with classroom notes and translations. All in ink. Not ballpoint ink. *Ink.* I used to spend weary evenings trying to erase the worst of the mess without rubbing holes in the cheap paper.

Never mind. Bad as they were, the books didn't have to be taken back to the library just as I was beginning to understand them. By 1948, my shelves were full and I was considering adding another orange crate, when all of us in the bed-sitter building got eviction notices. The building was to be gutted and remodelled.

A friend took my books in — I didn't own much else — and with a suitcase in one hand and my typewriter in the other, I set out, in the teeth of a postwar housing shortage, to hunt for a place to live. After eighteen months of wandering — of two-week and two-month sublets for a total of eleven addresses and phone numbers and mail that took months to catch up with me — I finally found a dark little converted apartment in a house in a quiet row on East 95th Street. A friend built me long bookshelves from wooden slats and crates he found in the building's cellar, I painted them (and everything else in sight) with shiny white enamel, and on a September day in '49 I finally moved into a clean, bright, makeshift apartment that was all mine. Two days later my books came home. As I put them up on their shiny shelves, I told them I was finally going to see that they were properly clothed in decent editions.

A few nights later I was reading the bookstore ads in the Out-of-print Books column of the *Saturday Review of Literature*. There was a whole column of out-of-print bookstores in New York I hadn't known about (having spent my time with friends more interested in Broadway and Hollywood than in English classics). I got a pencil and was circling the names of those that seemed most likely to have the books I wanted, when my eye fell on an ad lower down in the column:

Marks & Co., Antiquarian Booksellers
84, Charing Cross Road
London WC 2

London had held a special glamour for me from the time when I was eight or nine and my parents began taking me to the theatre. London was *The Barretts of Wimpole Street* and *Berkeley Square* and *Pygmalion*. It was also *Private Lives* and *Design for Living* because whether Noël Coward's characters were disporting themselves in Paris or on the Riviera, you knew they lived in Mayfair.

Then Q brought English literature into my life and my passion for London grew. Sam Pepys's London might be gone, but Leigh Hunt's was still there. I wanted to take the walks he took at night. I wanted to stand on Westminster Bridge and look at the view, because Wordsworth said Earth had not anything to show more fair. But it was all day-dreaming. Between my hand-to-mouth income and my fear of travel, I never really expected to see London. Staring at that ad, I thought it would be a lovely consolation prize to hold in my hands books that actually came from there. Marks & Co. might be another Chaucer Head, but while I was afraid to walk into such a bookshop I wasn't afraid to write a letter to one. I wrote to Marks & Co., requesting three books and warning the shop that I couldn't pay more than five dollars for each of them.

Someone at Marks & Co. — the letter was signed with the initials FPD — wrote back that two of the books I wanted were in stock and were being sent to me, for much less than five dollars each. And when they came in the mail I couldn't believe them. They were more appealing to me than the volumes in Chaucer Head's window — old, mellow leather-bound books with thick cream-colored pages, but not so opulently fine as to make me feel guilty if I underlined a phrase here (in pencil) or made a margin note there when I felt like it. They didn't have the look of rare or fine books, they looked like the friends I needed them to be. For a while I just stood, turning the pages of each, and I knew I'd never look anywhere else for books.

I was between plays that fall. If you're a writer with nothing in the typewriter and time on your hands, you write something — anything — just to keep from going crazy. I began writing long, goofy letters to Marks & Co., addressing them first to FPD and then, when I finally wormed his name out of him, to Frank Doel, who handled all my book orders. Then one of the girls in the shop began slipping personal notes in with the books she mailed to me. By which time I'd learned about England's food rationing. I began sending food parcels to the shop at Christmas and Easter, and all the people who worked in the shop wrote to thank me, and so did Frank Doel's wife, Nora, who told me about their two daughters, Sheila and Mary. So by

1952, when I broke into television as a writer of dramatic scripts, my correspondence with Marks & Co. was a part of my life. And the beautiful books kept coming.

As the Fifties wore on, and I wrote more and better-paid TV scripts, I began to regard a trip to London as a distinct future possibility and I kept threatening the shop with a visit. The only dream that took precedence over a trip to London was of one day living in a real apartment in a real apartment house. And eight years after the first one, a second eviction notice arrived in my mailbox. But this time I had a solid bank account and the prospect of earning more and more money writing for television.

On a spring morning, I went around to Second Avenue where, on the corner of 72nd Street, a new apartment house was under construction. It would be months before the building was finished, but there was a rental office on the ground floor, and sitting in that rental office with the building plans spread out before me, I signed a three-year lease on an apartment that wasn't there yet. But the floor plan indicated a large living room with a small alcove opening off it, a bathroom adjoining the alcove and a complete kitchen just off the foyer inside the front door.

In the six months before the building was finished, I blew my entire bank account on the first real furniture I ever owned. Only the best would do, especially for the alcove where I'd be working all day: a teak desk, an English walnut telephone table and walnut-stained bookshelves with small cabinet drawers below them, to run the length of the long back wall. I bought living-room furniture and wall-to-wall carpeting, and grey wool custom-made drapes to cover the long picture window and keep out the glare of street lights.

Herbie, the carpet-layer, unpacked all the furniture for

me and helped me put it all in place. When he left, I went into the kitchen, with its gleaming new white refrigerator and sink and cabinets, and carefully stripped the brown paper off the shining new stove. Then I took a bath in my first real tile bathroom. I spent the evening sitting first in the deep armchair, then in the modern Swedish rocker, to feast my eyes on the living room. Then I curled up on the carpet in the middle of the room and stared at the rows of books looking so proud on their first real bookshelves on the alcove wall. And when I took a last long look around the room before crawling into bed that night, I said aloud:

"It's a palace."

(After all these years it's still a palace to me. I clean it every Saturday, to wake up in a Sunday-clean house, and I still sometimes come home late on a Saturday night in winter, close the door behind me and lean against it, to stare at the freshly polished furniture, warm brown against the grey carpet and drapes, and think: "Isn't it beautiful?")

But now that I was a proper householder I found more expenses cropping up: a vacuum cleaner; complete sets of china and silverware that didn't come from Woolworth's; handsome new towels befitting my handsome 3-by-5 bathroom. So it was a couple of years before I could start saving for the trip to London. I set my sights on the summer of 1960.

In the late winter of 1959, the TV show I was writing for went off the air. In the spring no new assignments were offered me. In the summer of 1960, I woke up and realized that the entire television production industry had pulled up stakes and moved to Hollywood. The era of live TV had ended. From then on, dramatic television shows would be filmed like movies. Most of my fellow TV writers had already followed their careers to California. But Hollywood isn't a place, it's a way of life. And it wasn't for me.

I spent the summer searching the *Times* Help Wanted columns for jobs open to writers. There were jobs listed for ad agency copywriters, medical writers, writers with degrees in the sciences, writers with experience on magazines or in publishing offices. I was secretly relieved not to qualify for any of them. Better to starve at home than wither and die in an office prison. But I had to fight a sense of panic. I couldn't see how I was to earn a living for the rest of my life.

Early in the following winter my agent called to ask if I had any old plays or TV scripts she might sell to West German television. She told me what they were looking for and I got a few TV scripts down from the closet shelf and the only two plays that hadn't gone down the incinerator. I'd kept both for sentimental reasons.

One was about life at the Theatre Guild and the backstage story of *Oklahoma!* Looking at it, I remembered what one producer had said when he rejected it.

"This isn't a play," he told me. "It might make a good magazine article."

"That's prose," I thought, staring at it. "I can't write prose." And an old line dropped into my head:

"To the writer of good honest prose, these notions are about as useful as the wind in the next street."

Where had I read that? Oh, Q. He was talking about German literary criticism, if I remembered right. I probably didn't. I hadn't read Q in years. And then I think my mouth fell open. *Q!* How many years had I sweated through his lectures on how to write prose? How many models of English prose had he sent me to that I'd loved for years, including Hunt and Lamb and Hazlitt, and what were all their essays but magazine articles reprinted later in books?

And I thought I could hear Q remarking that possibly I couldn't write prose, but with the rent coming due every month it might be advisable to try.

It took me two weeks to convert the Theatre Guild play to a magazine article and when I finished it I mailed it to *Harper's Magazine*. Then I reread the second play and I spent another two weeks converting that one into a magazine article. With beginner's luck, I sold the first to *Harper's* and the second to *The New Yorker*. So of course I spent the rest of the winter and spring writing thirteen more magazine articles I couldn't sell anywhere. I was very broke by June when the *Harper's* article finally appeared. A few days later a letter arrived in the mail from Harper & Row, Publishers.

Dear Miss Hanff:

This is just to tell you how much I enjoyed your story about the Theatre Guild in this month's Harper's.

Do you have a book in mind?

Sincerely,
Genevieve Young

I wrote to Miss Young, explaining that I was a TV writer and didn't have a book in mind. But when she got the letter, she phoned and said why didn't we have lunch anyway? and we set a date for Friday of the following week. Maybe by that time, she said, one of us would have thought of a book for me to write.

I spent that week in a sweat that had nothing to do with the summer heat. In spite of the hundreds of bad ones I'd suffered through as a professional reader, I was in awe of people who wrote books. But now that the suggestion had been made, I itched to try writing one — and found there was no kind of book whatsoever I was equipped to write. I didn't like novels. (I subscribe to Randall Jarrell's definition of a novel as "a prose narrative that has something wrong with it.") I had no qualifications for writing history or biography. And having neither literary reputation nor Palace connections, I was in no position to write the kind of book I most loved to read: memoirs, diaries, letters. I flogged my brain to try and think of anything I could suggest to Genevieve Young. Nothing came.

I dressed very carefully for the lunch, to give myself a veneer of confidence. Hong Kong dresses were still fashionable, and I'd bought a brown linen one at Saks the summer before, which still looked chic. It was a beautiful day and I wanted to walk down to Harper's, but I didn't. I wore the white high-heeled pumps that hurt, and took a Madison Avenue bus. The bus was nearly empty, but I stood all the way to 33rd Street so as not to crease the linen. I got off the bus in front of Harper's, took the elevator up to the editorial floor and gave my name to the receptionist. And when she phoned it in and told me Miss Young would be right out, I draped myself negligently on a chair arm (to avoid stomach creases in the dress) and waited.

My only consolation, when she came out, was that even she knew the name "Genevieve" was too fussy for her. The first thing she said — after "Hi" — was "Call me Gene." She was a head taller than I was, she had jet-black hair and a beautiful face, she was regally poised, she was Chinese — and the beige silk Hong Kong dress she wore had been made for her. In Hong Kong. ("My sister lives there.") Its slit skirt in no way impeded her long-legged stride toward the elevator, and as I stepped in beside her she towered over me, which the Chinese are not supposed to do. We went next door to a hotel dining room where she strode to her regular table. I pattered along behind her, feeling small, round-shouldered and inferior.

We settled opposite each other and ordered lunch. As the waiter departed, Gene hopped a little in her chair and said:

"I've got a great idea for your book! Why don't you write a funny book about everything that's happened to you since you first came to New York to crash the theatre?"

Warmth flooded through me and I was glad she was tall and beautiful and had genuine Hong Kong dresses and enough assurance for both of us.

"I could write that," I said.

I spent the next six months writing the story of my life for Gene (and $1,500), and since the construction was all wrong I had to spend another six months rewriting it. The book, called *Underfoot in Show Business*, crept out during a New York newspaper strike, got mildly approving reviews in other cities, took a few years to sell its 5,000 copies and then (the only thing it ever had in common with the books I loved) went out of print. And I embarked on a decade-long battle to keep the rent paid.

I wrote training films for the Women's Army Corps, I wrote articles on American history for a children's encyclopedia, I wrote a couple of children's bedtime stories. Month after month I worried about the rent and had bad dreams at night, of a third and final eviction notice; but by some miracle I managed to keep the rent paid and the palace roof over my head without borrowing money.

Every few months Gene Young phoned. Gene is telepathic and her phone calls always came when I was out of work. I'd say hello and Gene would say, without even the preamble of hello:

"What are you doing? Are you eating? I worry about you." Or: "I'm just checking up on you, are you writing anything?"

Between assignments I went doggedly on, trying to write magazine articles. (I am extremely bull-headed. It took twenty years of trying before I acknowledged I couldn't write a producible play. Magazine articles were this decade's plays.) Whenever I wrote one, Gene read it and told me what magazine and editor to send it to ("Use my name"). When it came back, as it always did, she said: "Meet me for lunch."

She thought of another book for me to write and got me another $1,500 in advance. When I finished the book it was dull and pointless and we both knew it had to go down the incinerator. And I couldn't return Harper's $1,500, having flung it all away recklessly on food and rent.

Then, in the mid-Sixties, I began to get fairly steady work writing short American history books for children. Each book paid a thousand dollars — no royalties — and each took me two to three months to research and write; and since this was a very good way to starve to death, I went back to reading scripts for a film studio, this time United Artists.

Now among the children's history book assignments was one about the founding of the Virginia and Massachusetts colonies. Both had bored me when I was a child. All I remembered of the New England settlement was Longfellow's *Courtship of Miles Standish* and how Miles Standish's emissary, John Alden, proposed to Priscilla in Standish's name and was told to "Speak for yourself, John."

I was even more bored by the Virginia myth of Pocahontas laying her head on the block to save Captain John Smith from being beheaded by the Indians (who didn't behead their victims and wouldn't have had the slightest idea what a "block" was). And to an eight- or ten-year-old, all the early settlers seemed to have come up out of the sea, from nowhere.

I went to the library and brought home a load of history books. Chapter I of the first book I opened was a wooden account of investors in London putting up money for the first expedition to "Virginia" — the name Englishmen in 1620 gave to the entire North American continent. I spent an evening copying out dreary lists of ships' supplies and the names of shipowners and investors. One investor's name, George Carteret, rang a faint bell, and I tried to remember where I'd heard it before. Then I gave it up and went to bed. I was drifting off to sleep when a line of print, literally, appeared inside my eyelids:

"Dined with Sir G. Carteret."

I sat bolt upright and shouted into the darkness:

"Pepys!"

I got out of bed, turned on the lights and got down Pepys from the bookshelf. I knew the diary began thirty-five years after the first settlements and though I sat huddled in a down quilt reading every mention of Sir G. Carteret listed in the index, I couldn't find out whether he was the investor or the investor's son. It didn't matter. Suddenly the world the investors lived in was real to me; it was the end of Shakespeare's world and the beginning of John Donne's. It was moving inexorably toward Milton's and Cromwell's Puritan world, which took root first in Massachusetts.

A few days later I went berserk with excitement to read that one of my book's heroes, Roger Williams, the Father of American Religious Liberty, had been the protégé of the great jurist Sir Edward Coke, "in whose house he was ever treated as a son," according to Coke's daughter. What did I need with Priscilla and her "Speak-for-yourself-John?" I had a young heretic named Roger Williams fleeing persecution at the hands of the Star Chamber, whose most rabid heretic-hunter was his foster father, Sir Edward Coke.

If all this history has been boring you to tears, you're not alone. I was spending my evenings at the time working in political campaigns at the local Democratic Club, and I couldn't wait to share all this exciting history with everybody at the club. Well, even the club lawyers listened glassy-eyed with boredom. But a few days later, Gene Young made one of her periodic phone calls.

"What are you doing, are you eating?"

"I'm writing an American history book for children," I said.

"You are?" said Gene, with such interest I thought she'd misunderstood me.

"It's for kids!" I repeated. "Aged eight to ten."

"I want to take you to lunch," said Gene. "How about Friday? Pick me up at the office at one."

I picked her up and we went to lunch. As soon as we'd ordered, Gene said:

"Tell me about the history book."

"It's about the early settlers of Virginia and Massachusetts," I said. "Pocahontas-and-all-that, but I've discovered —"

And Gene interrupted, with lordly assurance:

"Oh, I know all about Pocahontas. Somebody else was in love with her and she said, 'Speak for yourself, Miles Standish.'"

When I recovered, I stared at her beautiful face and asked:

"Where did you go to school?"

And Gene said:

"I went to kindergarten in Shanghai, to first grade in London, second and third grades in Paris and fourth grade in Manila."

She told me her father had been a diplomat for Nationalist China. She was born in Geneva — which is why they named her Genevieve — in the Thirties. ("My father was a delegate to the Second Opium Conference.") "Pearl Harbor happened when I was in the fifth grade in Manila," she went on. "The Japanese invaded the Philippines right afterwards. They interned all the Chinese diplomats, including my father. We didn't find out for sure until the war ended, but they executed them all."

Gene and her mother and two sisters were confined in a house with the women of other diplomatic families.

"The mothers organized a school for us. The local teachers taught us the history of the Philippines, an old man — the only Chinese male the Japanese hadn't killed — tried to teach us Chinese, and the servants taught us all the dirty words in Tagalog."

At the end of the war, Gene's mother brought her daughters to the United States on her diplomatic passport. Gene was enrolled in a fashionable boarding school where her Philippine education put her at a peculiar disadvantage.

"On my first day at Abbot Academy, the headmistress told me I would have to 'set an example' because I was the only Asian in the school," Gene said drily. "How could I tell her I'd never learned the Pledge of Allegiance to the flag? We didn't recite it very often anyway, and when we did the whole school recited it together and I just mumbled through it and came in strong on 'With liberty and justice for all.' "

"Do you know it now?" I asked.

"Where would I learn it?" she demanded. "I mumbled through it for four years at Wellesley, too."

I said that not knowing it didn't exactly blight her life. Gene said flatly:

"It could! I've applied for American citizenship. At the end of my probationary period, they give me a citizenship test. I don't know what the questions will be."

She showed me her Green Card, certifying her a legal alien, and she showed me the list of requirements for making it through the five-year probationary period. Her Green Card could be revoked if she

(a) broke the law by so much as a traffic violation.

(b) belonged to a "subversive" organization.

(c) committed adultery.

There were ten or twelve other requirements, all of them prohibiting acts Gene would be perfectly free to commit once she became a citizen.

For the next few months we met regularly. I was writing books for two children's history series and I poured all my research into Gene's tensely interested ears. In the spring of 1968, she phoned to report that she'd been given a date for her immigration hearing. It would include an interview, a literacy test and a citizenship test.

"Friends of mine have already taken it," she said, "and they told me the citizenship test is confined to one question. It can be about anything — the Constitution, the Supreme Court, anything!" Then she said: "I have to take two character witnesses with me to the hearing. Will you be one of them?"

"Of course I'll be one of them. I'm your coach!" I said.

On the appointed morning, I met Gene and her worried-looking second witness, Dolores, at a subway station for the trip to the courthouse in Brooklyn. I wore my best suit, Dolores wore her best dress. Gene, who had given up Hong Kong dresses for monotone sweaters-and-pants, wore a grey cashmere sweater, matching grey wool pants and a wide suede belt that was just a shade darker. With her glossy black hair piled high, she was a walking definition of the word "svelte." Dolores, who was a Harper's copy editor, was small and bespectacled like me, and behind her glasses her eyes were wide with apprehension. She was convinced that one wrong word from her during the hearing would get Gene instantly deported to Communist China.

All the way to Brooklyn we shouted questions at Gene over the screech of the subway.

"BILL OF RIGHTS?" shouted Dolores.

"FIRST TEN AMENDMENTS. I KNOW THEM!" said Gene.

"ELECTORAL COLLEGE?" I shouted. And Gene shouted back:

"WHAT ABOUT IT?"

We arrived at the courthouse, hoarse and tense, and took seats in a large room full of Hungarian refugees and exiled Croatians, Ukrainians and Armenians. All of them looked tired, grey-faced and shabby — and not one of them seemed as frightened of the coming ordeal as we were.

Gene's number was called and the three of us filed into a small cubbyhole to one side of the main room. A young immigration officer sat behind a desk. A court clerk lined us up in front of the desk and we all raised our right hands like three overage Girl Scouts and solemnly swore to tell the truth. Then the clerk departed and the three of us were left facing the immigration officer. After a morning of downtrodden immigrants from Mittel-Europa, he was eyeing the tall, chic Chinese and her two small decorous protectors with fascinated disbelief.

He told Gene and me to wait outside while he questioned Dolores, and we went back to the main room and sat. After ten minutes Dolores came out (very pale) and told me to go in. I went into the private office, and the young immigration officer asked me how long I'd known Gene and how much I knew about her. I gave her a glowing character reference and then he dismissed me and told me to send Gene in. Gene went in alone for her citizenship test. And Dolores and I sat and waited.

When Gene came out she looked strained, but she didn't report on the test till the three of us were out in the hall.

"I don't know whether I passed or not," she said. "First he pushed a pencil and paper at me and said: 'Write *The cat ran down the street*.' I'd forgotten about the literacy test. And I was so rattled I said: 'The what did what?' And he said: 'You're a Harper's editor and a Wellesley graduate and you can't spell cat?' "

The citizenship test question was: What is a pocket veto?

"I knew what it was, but he questioned me about the history of it and when a president uses it, and I'm not sure I knew enough to pass."

We were huddled in the hall, anxiously trading information about pocket vetoes, when the young immigration officer came out of his cubbyhole and headed for the elevator. Then he stopped, hesitated, turned and walked slowly back to us — and for half a minute I stopped breathing.

"If you're going to lunch," he said, "Sam Wu's is the best Chinese restaurant in Brooklyn." And he told us how to find it.

In June, Gene was notified that she had been granted citizenship and was to go back to the courthouse for her swearing-in. She phoned me when she got home and I said:

"Congratulations. How was it?"

"I wasted a lot of worry. It was okay," said Gene. "There were two hundred of us and the judge who administered it had us all recite the Pledge of Allegiance together. So I just mumbled through it and came in strong on 'With liberty and justice for all.'" And she added: "He was a nice old thing; he was having so much trouble with his new dental plate he wouldn't have noticed my lips didn't move."

I wrote another book for her that year. I left it at her office and she phoned the next day and said bluntly:

"I read it. It doesn't work."

I sat down and read it myself and saw Gene was right. The book went down the incinerator. I was still reading scripts for United Artists, but even with an occasional children's book I was earning so little that I managed to hang onto my apartment and stay out of debt only by buying nothing I didn't absolutely need. And I didn't absolutely need to own more books.

Then, in September of '69, I got an assignment to write a full-length book for teenagers on the young reformers of the Sixties. With money coming in I decided to splurge on a set of Jane Austen for my best friend, whose birthday was coming at the end of October; and for the first time in two years I wrote to Frank Doel. ("Still there, are we?" I began. And Frank wrote back: "Yes, we're all still here.")

He had no Austen to sell me, which turned out to be a blessing because the teenagers' book took much longer than I'd expected and by December, when I began the final draft of the book, I was very low in funds. I thought I'd better phone the editors of the two children's history series and get an assignment for February.

Both greeted me warmly on the phone, not having heard from me in six months. And in my memory, both broke the same news to me in the same words:

"Oh, we're not publishing the history series anymore. These kids won't read history; they say it's not relevant."

That evening I tried to take stock of myself and my future, but there seemed no stock to take. I was a failed playwright, a TV writer whose experience in live TV was useless in an age of film and a writer of children's history books nobody was publishing anymore. I was nowhere. I was nothing.

In January, revisions of the Sixties book staved off the blank future for a few more weeks. Early one morning I left the house to spend the day going from library to library in search of transcripts of Southern civil rights trials. It was nearly six when I finally walked into the lobby and stopped in the mail room to pick up my mail. I had an armload of books and I went through the mail that lay on top of them as I rode up in the elevator. Among the pile of bills and throwaways was the familiar thin blue envelope from Marks & Co.

There was something wrong with it. Frank Doel always typed the name and address single-spaced and always spelled out my first name. On this envelope the typing was double-spaced and the letter was addressed to "Miss H. Hanff." I thought:

"He's left the shop."

I was tired and depressed and the wrong-looking letter threatened to depress me further. I put it on the table and decided it would wait till after dinner. I made myself a rare and extravagant martini and worked a *Guardian Weekly* crossword puzzle as I drank it. And the letter waited.

I cooked dinner and went on working the crossword puzzle as I ate. Then I poured a cup of coffee and lit a cigarette. Feeling more cheerful ("If he's left the shop, you can always write to him and Nora at home, you have their address"), I reached for the blue airmail letter.

8th January, 1969.

Dear Miss,

I have just come across the letter you wrote to Mr. Doel on the 30th of September last, and it is with great regret that I have to tell you that he passed away on Sunday the 22nd of December, the funeral took place on Wednesday, the 1st of January.

The death has been a very great shock to Mr. Cohen, especially coming so soon after the death of Mr. Marks.

⇛ TWO ⇚

"They've Shot Goldberg"

AT ANY TIME, the news of Frank's death would have been a grief to me, and the one death too many among those I'd loved without ever meeting them. (I'd been working in the presidential campaign of Robert Kennedy when he was murdered, two months after the murder of Martin Luther King.) Coming when it did, the news was devastating. It seemed to me that with the double loss of Frank Doel and Mr. Marks, the last anchor in my life — my bookshop — was being taken from me. I began to cry and I couldn't stop. I don't know at what point in my crying I began to mutter over and over:

"I have to write it."

Then I stopped crying abruptly and went cold inside. I could only write it if I still had Frank's letters.

I'd begun saving them twenty years earlier because a tax accountant wanted a record of what I spent on books. When he discovered I spent too little for a sizable tax deduction he lost interest, but I'd got into the habit of saving them by that time and I went on doing it. The thin blue airmail letters with a rubber band around them took up no space, lying nearly flat under manuscripts in a back corner of one of the six small cabinet drawers under my bookshelves. But year after year when I cleaned out the cabinets, I'd come on them and wonder why I was saving them. Sitting there that evening, I vividly remembered that when I'd reorganized the cabinets a few weeks earlier I'd stood by the waste basket hefting the letters, debating whether to keep them or throw them out. I couldn't remember which I'd done. And I was afraid to find out.

I carried the dinner tray to the kitchen and washed the dishes. I mopped the kitchen floor, emptied the garbage, wiped the dinner table. Then I poured another cup of coffee. The letters had become terribly important; they had to be there. Finally, I made myself get up and walk to the cabinet by the window where I'd always kept them. I opened the drawer and reached in the back corner. They weren't there. I pulled out the drawer and hunted through the papers in it, but the letters were gone.

I looked in the second cabinet and then, with mounting irrational panic, through the next three. I came to the sixth and last drawer — a catchall attic of a cabinet — and in my anxiety yanked it clear out of the wall unit. And there, in a back corner, was the familiar flat blue packet. I sat down on the floor and cried with relief. (Part of my mind was demanding "What's the matter with you? Why is it so important?")

I carried the letters to the table and opened them — and snapshots of young families spilled out of them. Some were from Nora Doel, some were from one of the girls who worked in the shop, all of them were ten or fifteen years in the past. I found two letters from an old lady named Mrs. Boulton who lived next door to the Doels. They'd persuaded her to sell one of her hand-embroidered luncheon cloths to the bookshop staff to send me, one Christmas.

("I don't usually part with any of my work," she'd written when she got my letter telling her how beautiful it was.) I found snapshots of Frank standing proudly beside his new secondhand car. I was laughing by this time. I poured another cup of coffee and settled down to read the letters.

By the time I went to bed I was positively happy. I was going to relive the lovely episode Marks & Co. had been in my life by making a short story of the correspondence. *The New Yorker* sometimes published short stories in the form of letters and if I constructed the story properly they just might buy it.

But when I finished the story in March, it ran sixty-seven pages, more than three times the length of the only story I'd ever sold to *The New Yorker,* and I didn't know where else to send it.

When in doubt, send it to Gene.

The story had no title so I put a sheet of paper in the typewriter and typed the address of the bookshop — 84, Charing Cross Road — as a stopgap title. The title would make no sense at all to Americans, but magazine editors always change authors' titles to suit themselves so it didn't matter. I put the story in an envelope and mailed it to Gene with a one-line note:

"What do I do with this?"

A few days later the phone rang and when I said hello, a familiar, forthright voice said:

"I loved it, I cried. Why do you always send me things I can't publish?"

"It's too long for *The New Yorker,*" I said. "I thought you could tell me where to send it."

I heard Gene sigh.

"Let me think about it," she said. A week or two went by before she called me back.

"Our sales manager is an antiquarian book dealer on the side," she said. "So I gave him your manuscript to read. And he said to me: 'I love it. But if you're thinking of publishing it, I have to tell you it's not gonna sell.' So then I went to the top and gave it to Cass Canfield, the chairman of our board. And he said: 'It's charming. But it's terribly slight. And it's letters. You know letters don't sell.' "

"Well, who told you it was a book?" I said impatiently. "It's sixty-seven pages! I just thought you might know some literary quarterly I could send it to. It's too long for the only magazines I read."

"That's the trouble with it," said Gene. "It's too short for a book and too long for a magazine article. It doesn't fit anywhere."

She returned it to me and it lay on my desk for a couple of weeks. It was still there one night when Maia Gregory phoned. Maia was the United Artists story editor for whom I read a few novels a week. She lived in the building next door to mine and she phoned that night and said, as usual:

"Come on over; I have work for you."

I hung up and started for the door. Then I had a thought. I went back to the desk, picked up the manuscript and took it with me; and when Maia handed me the galleys of a novel to read, I handed her the manuscript and said:

"Do me a favor. Whenever you get time, will you read this thing and put an X against every letter I can cut? I want to send it to a magazine and it's much too long."

"Oh, goody, I have something to read in bed," said Maia.

I went home and read the galleys, and after breakfast the next morning got to work on my reader's report. I was halfway through it when Maia phoned.

"I know one publisher who just might be crazy enough

to publish this," she said. "I'm having lunch with him. Can I give it to him?"

"Sure," I said. We hung up and I went back to my reader's report. Two weeks went by. Then the phone rang one morning and a pleasant baritone at the other end said:

"Miss Hanff? This is Dick Grossman"

— and waited, obviously expecting the name to mean something to me. It didn't, and he added: "Your publisher."

"I don't have a publisher named Dick Grossman," I said blankly. And he said:

"You do now. We're going to publish '84, Charing Cross Road.'"

"In what?" I asked.

"As a book," said Dick Grossman. And I said:

"You're crazy!"

A few days later I went down to Grossman Publishers for a story conference. Dick Grossman operated a small publishing house out of an old, spacious stone house on East 19th Street, with high ceilings and a fireplace in every room. He published slim, offbeat volumes — Ben Shahn, a new translation of Catullus, James Lipton's *An Exaltation of Larks*. (Dick left the publishing business a year or two later and it was a genuine loss; there were and are few like him.) Dick's editor wanted to read any of Frank's letters I'd omitted and when he read them he wanted all of them included, together with answers from me, and eventually the book ran ninety pages, which was a little more respectable. (In my excitement I forgot to tell him that a London street address would mean nothing to American readers and that we needed a new title. For the rest of my life I was going to be told by neighbors and fellow dinner-guests how much they'd enjoyed my book "64 Charring Road" or "47 Crossroads.")

Dick Grossman wanted to bring out the book in the fall of 1970 (it was too late for his fall '69 list), and in the catalogue he sent out early in July, the book was listed for September publication. That catalogue was responsible for the last blue envelope that would ever come in the mail from Marks & Co.

Dear Miss Hanff,

We have just learned that your book '84, Charing Cross Road,' is listed in Grossman's catalogue of publications for August.

You will be sorry to learn that owing to a redevelopment scheme, these premises are due for demolition in the near future. So after fifty years in the Charing Cross Road, we will be closing down at the end of this year.

As well as being a tribute to the firm, your book will, in a way, be its obituary.

Fortunately, I was too busy that summer to mourn the bookshop. I was president of the Democratic Club and we were heavily involved in the gubernatorial campaign of former Supreme Court Justice Arthur Goldberg. It was the first campaign I'd worked in since Bobby Kennedy's death, and through the summer and on into September I was preoccupied with it.

On a Friday morning in September, therefore, while everybody else was reading the morning *Times* over breakfast, I was studying a list of election districts that still needed workers — unaware that the morning *Times* carried a two-column review of *84, Charing Cross Road*, which began: "This is a charmer." I was pencilling in names of potential E.D. captains, when, at a little before eight, the phone rang. At that hour it could only be a club member reporting some new crisis. Sure enough, when I said Hello, Bill, one of the club regulars, was at the other end. How was I to know he was looking at a book review?

"Hi," he said. I said:

"What's the matter?"

"Have you seen the *Times?*"

"No," I said. "What's happened?"

"Are you sitting down?" asked Bill.

And with 1968 rushing back to me, I thought:

"My God, they've shot Goldberg!"

Only Chicken Little would believe what happened to me from then on. First, reviews began coming in from all over the country, so glowing I couldn't believe them. Then it was bought for reprint by the *Reader's Digest,* and the *Digest* check — $8,000, which I also couldn't believe — put me back on my financial feet for the first time in ten years.

The book appealed to only a small percentage of readers so its sales were what publishers politely call "modest." But what its readers lacked in numbers they made up for in fanaticism. It wasn't till a couple of years later that I first read in a trade paper that *84* was known to the publishing trade as "a Cult book," but from the beginning that's what it was.

If you write a Cult book — and your current address is printed at the top of the last dozen pages of it — and your phone number is listed in the Manhattan phone book, the Cult loses no time getting in touch with you.

Every morning when I went down for the mail, the little steel cubbyhole mailbox was so stuffed with fan letters I had to pry them out in sections. Some began: "Dear Helene. I hope you don't mind me calling you that. I feel as if I know you." Some of them moved me to tears. And one began simply:

Dear Miss Hanff:

Would you consider marrying a fifteen-year-old boy with terminal acne?

I answered every letter and saved them all carefully in a shoebox — which became two shoeboxes and then three, all bursting out of shape as more and more letters were crammed into them. Once, in a temporary fit of common sense, I considered throwing each letter away as I answered it, but the thought shocked me. It seemed so coldly ungrateful and God knew I wasn't.

It was a pity I couldn't keep the phone calls in a shoebox.

The first few were ordinary enough. Readers in New York or in some Jersey or Connecticut suburb finished the book, reached for the phone and got my number from the operator, finding it quicker and more satisfying to talk to me than to write to me.

The first flatly incredible call came on a hot September Saturday. I was on a ladder cleaning the kitchen cabinets clad chiefly in sweat, when the phone rang. I sprinted down the ladder, streaked across the living room, picked up the phone and — so as not to offend whichever friend was at the other end — said, very fast:

"I'm housecleaning the kitchen, I'll call you back, who is it?" And a man at the other end said imploringly:

"Oh, please don't hang up! It's taken us three hours to

get through to you. We're calling from Prince George, British Columbia."

He and his wife had planned a weekend holiday to celebrate the birth of their son, but at the last minute the holiday had been cancelled.

"We couldn't go away so we read your book instead. And it cheered us so much we thought we'd treat ourselves to a phone call."

"Why couldn't you go away?" I asked. And he said: "We're snowed in."

A woman phoned one evening from Lubbock, Texas, and said:

"We can talk as long as you're willing. The phone call is my husband's fortieth birthday present to me. He knew it was the one thing I wanted."

A woman phoned one morning from Alaska and apologized for the "intrusion."

"This must be costing you a fortune!" I said. "Why didn't you write to me instead?"

"I'm married to an Eskimo and we live three hundred miles from the nearest town," she said. "I didn't want to wait till spring when the roads clear and we can get into town to the post office."

A man called from San Francisco one Sunday afternoon — and from then on he phoned regularly, once a month, to ask how I was and what I was writing. And there was the inevitable fly-in-the ointment. Jay Schmidt.

Jay Schmidt phoned at dinner time one night and said he was calling from Texas, he was eighty-four, he had lung cancer but he felt fine — it was in remission — and he loved my book. He felt like talking and it was quite a while before I could get him to hang up so I could finish cooking dinner.

From then on, he called regularly once a week, always at dinner time. "Jay, I've got company coming in ten minutes and I'm not dressed," I'd say hurriedly. Or: "Jay, I'm halfway out the door, I'm going to a concert."

And each time, Jay would say:

"You haven't got five minutes to talk to an old man who's dying of lung cancer?"

He kept it up for two years. Then the phone calls stopped and I wished him Godspeed.

And there was the bitter winter night when the ringing phone got me out of bed at three in the morning and a young Hollywood composer said proudly:

"I've been up since six this morning but I made myself keep awake until midnight, so as not to call you before nine p.m. your time. I didn't want to interrupt your dinner."

I explained to him that he'd got the time difference backward, and I stood freezing by the open window for twenty minutes while he apologized abjectly and profusely for getting me out of bed, and told me how much *84* meant to him.

After the phone calls came the invitations. From total strangers.

"My friends and I are great admirers of your book and most anxious to meet you. I should like to give a luncheon for you at the Century Club on any Tuesday in November. Will you let me know which date is most convenient?"

"My husband and I are great fans of your book, so are three couples who live near us. I'd love to give a small dinner party for you on any Friday evening you name."

How do you write back and say that, like everybody else, you're too shy to walk into a roomful of strangers and make conversation with them while they stare at you?

A couple in Minnesota and another in Florida wrote months in advance to give me the date of their projected one-week trip to New York and ask which day of the week I'd be free for lunch or dinner. I dreaded spending a long dinner hour with strangers who might find me a crushing disappointment, but how do you write back in November that you're all booked up for the second week in February? I was totally unprepared for all this and I didn't know how to handle it.

There was an avalanche of Christmas cards from fans that first year. And a few days before Christmas a package arrived from Marks & Co. I opened it and found inside a first edition of *Daddy-Long-Legs* inscribed to me by Joan Todd, Frank Doel's secretary. When I turned the page I saw a second inscription. It was laboriously hand-printed in pencil on a torn scrap of paper taped to the page. It was written by the Marks & Co. shipping clerk. It read:

> This was the last parcel I packed up before the firm closed down.
>
> *Pat*

Shortly after the new year began, Dick Grossman phoned.

"André Deutsch wants to bring out *84* in London," he said. "He's one of England's best and most discriminating publishers. You couldn't ask for a better."

A few weeks later my agent phoned to say a contract had arrived from André Deutsch, setting publication date for June 1971 and offering two hundred pounds in advance of royalties. Without any forethought I heard myself say:

"Tell him to keep the money over there for me. I'm going over in June."

All these years later — now that Frank was dead and the bookshop closed — I was finally going to London.

Shortly before I was to leave, a retired actress gave a dinner party for me and over dinner she suggested I keep a diary while I was in London.

"So much will be happening to you," she said. "You think you'll remember it all but you won't."

Much as I loved reading diaries I'd never believed in keeping one; it was too much like talking to yourself. But that spring there was a fad in New York for something called "the Nothing book" — a clothbound book of empty pages — and the day before I left for London, a friend gave me one "so you can keep a diary in London."

I took a morning plane, landed at Heathrow at ten p.m. — and by midnight, so much had already happened to me that I sat on the edge of the bed and recorded the evening's events in the Nothing book. From then on, through five hectic, wide-eyed weeks in London, I made myself do this every night, no matter how late I got in or how tired I was. When I came home I typed the scrawled diary entries and put the bundle of typewritten sheets in a cabinet drawer, relieved to know I had a record of the trip to take out and read some day.

The London reviews were as glowing as the American ones, and I took a set to Gene Young one day when we met for lunch.

"You don't know what it does to me," I said, "that after being nursed along by you for ten years, I finally write a book that gets rave reviews in two countries — and it's published by somebody else."

"What it does to YOU!" said Gene with feeling. And I went home vowing to write a new book for her. For months I ransacked my mind for one. Nothing turned up.

A fresh ton of letters arrived from England and Australia. A few were from Londoners who had bought books from Marks & Co. One woman wrote that she had passed the shop one morning during the Battle of Britain, to find its windows had been blown out by the bombing the night before.

"The sidewalk was covered with shattered glass. But passersby had stopped and were picking books out of the gutter and putting them carefully back in the broken window."

There were letters from readers who had been children during the war and remembered "the arrival of the marvellous food parcels from America."

The fan mail kept coming all that winter and spring, much of it from England. On a June evening, remembering the previous June and wishing I were back in London, I got out the typewritten diary and settled in the armchair to read it and relive the trip.

"Whenever I write a letter to somebody, I mail it without reading it over," a fellow TV writer once told me. "I know if I read it over I'll start rewriting it."

I hadn't read a paragraph of that diary before I had to get a pencil and rewrite a sentence to clarify it. Three hours later, when I went to bed, I'd only read through the first two days' entries — and both were so heavily marked up I knew I'd have to retype them in the morning if I ever hoped to read them again.

As I ate breakfast the next morning, it occurred to me that if I rewrote the diary and cut it, I might be able to sell it to a travel magazine. At nine o'clock I put paper in the typewriter and got to work. And at ten o'clock my telepathic friend phoned.

Gene had been busy moving from the suburbs to the

city and from Harper's to Lippincott and I hadn't talked to her in several months. When I picked up the phone and said hello, she said:

"I just thought I'd find out what you're doing."

"An hour ago I started rewriting the diary I kept in London," I said. "I thought maybe —"

"You're writing another book!" said Gene. "This one's mine!"

I looked at the paper in the typewriter. I was on page 4 and I hadn't even got as far as the first entry, I was just writing an introduction. Okay, I was writing another book.

During the next several months Gene phoned every few weeks for a progress report. Late on a Friday afternoon in November, I took the last page out of the typewriter and without stopping to stack the pages, dialed her number. When she came to the phone I said:

"Wanna buy a book?"

"You finished it!" said Gene. "Bring it down."

"I have to proofread it; I'll bring it down Monday," I said.

"I'll proofread it. Bring it down now."

"I have to shower and change and it's after four. I couldn't get down there by five anyway!" I said.

"Get down when you can. I'll wait," said Gene.

I got to Lippincott's at five-thirty and there was nobody in the place but Gene. We Xeroxed the manuscript and then we went to Schrafft's to celebrate. (Schrafft's — a chain of tearoomy restaurants noted for its gooey desserts — was the only place where I could have my martini and Gene could have her hot butterscotch sundae with toasted almonds.)

On Friday night, Gene read the manuscript and on Saturday, she phoned to tell me she loved it.

47

On Monday, Lippincott's editor-in-chief read it and on Tuesday, Gene phoned to say triumphantly that the editor-in-chief liked it and Lippincott was going to publish it.

On Wednesday, the author read it. With increasing horror. On Wednesday afternoon, I phoned Gene.

"This thing is awful!" I said. "Garrulous Gertie comes home from London and has to tell everybody about her trip. Who the hell cares about my trip?"

"Everybody who read *84, Charing Cross Road,*" said Gene promptly. And it hit me with full force that my beloved Cult was going to rush out and buy this mess and I would die of shame.

In December, I made the few changes Gene wanted and a hundred hair-splitting changes of my own in an attempt to improve it. When the galleys came in January, I read them and discovered I hadn't improved anything.

"Lippincott's going to lose its shirt on this thing," I told Gene when I returned the galleys.

"Why are you worrying about Lippincott? They've got more money than you have," Gene pointed out reasonably. Then she said:

"It's going to be a rush job, we have an April publication date. You'll have to find me a new title in the next week or two."

"What's the matter with 'London Diary'?" I asked.

"It's a little less than compelling," said Gene in a withering tone. "I can't go to a sales conference with anything as dull as that!"

We'd mailed a copy of the manuscript to André Deutsch and my agent phoned to say he liked it and was going to publish it. I called Gene and told her and she said:

"I'll see him next week; I'm going to London on business. I'll tell him a new title's on the way. You'd better have one by the time I come home."

Gene had gone abroad a few years earlier and had regaled me later with a description of what she'd gone through, watching airport Immigration officials — in Amsterdam, in Rome, in Paris — pore over her Nationalist Chinese passport, turning it four ways, hoping to get it right-side-up, and finding they couldn't read a word of it in any direction. ("I couldn't help them," she'd explained apologetically. "I couldn't read it either.")

She was still away when the page-proofs of the book arrived in February, but when I went down to her office to return them a few days later, she was back behind her desk.

"How was the trip?" I asked.

"Great," said Gene. "I had a wonderful time in London."

"What was the high point?" I asked.

She looked at me and hesitated. Then she said:

"You won't believe it, but the high point came after I landed at JFK. It was mobbed and I was annoyed, I was tired and I had to stand on a long line at the Immigration desk. We inched along and finally I got to the desk and put my new passport on it, and the man behind the desk looked at it and stamped it. Then he pushed it back to me and said: 'Welcome home.' And I had tears in my eyes."

The alien with the Chinese passport was finally an ordinary American citizen coming home.

Which was as it should be, since the inside of Gene Young's head is about as Chinese as General Motors. She phoned me one evening and announced triumphantly:

"I've got the title for you!"

"What is it?" I asked.

" 'Son of 84, Charing Cross Road,' " said Gene.

I told her I'd see us both dead first. We finally settled on *The Duchess of Bloomsbury Street* (another long, wordy title nobody would ever get straight). But when the cover design arrived it featured a Lion and a Unicorn holding up a copy of *84, Charing Cross Road*. I phoned her the next morning.

"Did you really think I'd approve this cover?" I demanded.

"You don't have approval. I sent it as a courtesy," said General Motors. "Are you going to be home all afternoon? I'm sending a man up for your fan mail. We're getting out a special mailing to all your fans."

That afternoon the man from Lippincott carted off five shoeboxes full of fan mail. And that night or the next, I dreamed I was opening sad and accusing letters about the new book, from ex-fans who had trusted me.

In March, advance copies of the book were sent to "the trade" — reviewers, publishers, bookstore owners. I was tired of worrying about it by then, and wishing I had something new to write, when a letter came in the mail from Holt, Rinehart & Winston, Publishers. I'd never written anything for Holt, Rinehart, but they published school textbooks and I thought maybe they knew I'd written children's history books and were offering me work. I opened the letter and glanced down at the signature: "Tom Wallace, Editor-in-Chief." Then I read the first sentence — and my legs were suddenly so weak I had to sit down.

Dear Miss Hanff:

You've done it again . . .

He'd read an advance copy of *The Duchess of Blooms-bury Street.*

A few days later a letter came from the owner of a bookshop in a New York suburb.

Dear Miss Hanff:

You've done it again.

And it seemed to me that the Lord must be feeling guilty about what He'd put me through in the Sixties and was seeing to it that I could do nothing wrong in the Seventies.

The reviews were "mixed." I give you the last lines of two of them:

"This book is an act of love. I loved it."
— Neil Millar; *Christian Science Monitor*

"The book should never have been published."
— John Barkham; *San Francisco Chronicle*

(John Barkham was the dean of American reviewers, but he bounced right off Gene. "He's in the minority," she said. "The book's selling very well.")

Then the deluge of fan mail began pouring in from both countries. To my unspeakable relief, the Cult had not only survived My Trip but enjoyed it.

I'll never know a Christmas as wild as that one. Along with the blizzard of cards came gifts, including more books than I had room for.

There were books sent to me by their unknown authors, there were seventeen books about London and England, a few about Australia (from Australian fans) and, from a woman in Switzerland, the complete works of Washington

Irving in two-inch miniatures. There was a beautiful set of Jane Austen from a woman in Australia who wrote that she was getting old, she knew her children would sell her books when she died and she wanted her Austen in the hands of someone who would appreciate it. (At the time, *Pride and Prejudice* was the only Austen I owned; I'd read the others and hadn't liked any of them much. But if the donor is reading this, I want her to know that just last week I finished rereading all of the others in turn, not for the first time, and blessed her all over again for putting Jane's books so firmly on my shelves.)

And there was the truly awesome volume from the couple who owned an antique shop in upstate New York and who wrote that the book was worthless as an antique. It was a 1651 edition of John Donne's poems. I put it up on the shelf in a plastic sandwich bag because I was afraid to touch it. (It's still in the sandwich bag and I'm still afraid to touch it.)

Along with the books came the edibles and the unclassifiables. The edibles included pecans from Georgia, cheese from Wisconsin, homemade preserves from three young matrons in Oregon and an enormous box of grapefruit sent to me from Florida by a man who lived in Michigan. (He was only wintering in Florida and I had to phone the Florida fruit-seller and get the man's Michigan address so I could write and thank him.)

The unclassifiables included a plate with the raised head of Shakespeare on it; a Hanff family tree painted in oils; a yard of Nottingham lace; a miniature koala and a miniature Eskimo doll for my Christmas tree and a pair of skittles. (If you've read about "beer and skittles" and wondered what skittles were, mine are small varnished sticks about six inches long, smooth and rounded, with decorative knobs at each end. They could be the banister posts of a doll's-house staircase.)

Considering all of which, you'd think I'd have been grateful enough not to complain about the one fly in the Christmas ointment. I complained incessantly about it. It began late in November when I came home one afternoon and the doorman said:

"There's a package for you."

The package clearly contained a book and I carried it up-stairs with pleased anticipation. Then I opened it. It contained two books. Written by me. And a letter from a man in Boston:

> The enclosed books are part of my Christmas gift to my mother in Canada, to whom a personal inscription from you would mean so much. I enclose her name and address. And will you include a covering note to say the books are from her son Tad? (She doesn't call me Thomas.)

From then on, a similar package arrived in the mail room every day. One package contained two *84*'s and two *Duchesses*.

> The enclosed sets of your books are Christmas gifts. One set is to be autographed to my fiancé in Alabama, whose name and address I enclose, and the other is for my sister, Grace, and can be returned to me at the above address in Chicago.

> Enclosed please find your two books. They are for my son and daughter-in-law in Tel Aviv. Will you be kind enough to autograph them and then add Happy Hanukah from Mother? I enclose the postage.

Some enclosed the postage; some suggested I bill them for it. Nobody sent a stamped, self-addressed bookmailer. I had to run down to the stationery store for them, autograph the books, address and staple the bookmailers, lug them to the post office and stand in a Christmas line.

"Just mail them back where they came from!" an irate friend advised me.

But you can't do that to people — and I'd have had to stand in line at the post office just as long to return them.

My reward came a few days before Christmas with the arrival of the one gift I still prize above all others.

To understand the saga of that gift, you need to know that in the two and a half years since *84* had been published, I'd answered hundreds of fan letters and that while a few fans' names stuck in my memory, most of them didn't. You also need to know that I answer every letter off-the-top-of-my-head, commenting on what each letter-writer had written to me. Occasionally, I remember what I wrote in answer to a particular letter. Mostly I don't.

Well, six months before this particular Christmas, on a morning in July, I got a postcard from a New York couple who were vacationing in London. They wrote that they were fans of *84* and had gone around to Charing Cross Road to see the empty bookshop, which was still standing. And they added:

"We met your friend Dan Kelly from Omaha. He says to tell you he's getting the sign for you."

I didn't have a friend named Dan Kelly in Omaha, and I didn't know what sign he was talking about. Having no New York address for the writers of the postcard, I threw it away and forgot about it. Till a November evening when my phone rang and a pleasant male voice said:

"Hi! It's Dan Kelly in Omaha."

That brought the postcard to mind and I said — extra-cordially to cover my ignorance:

"Oh, how *are* you?"

"Fine," he said. "I've got the sign for you."

I couldn't bluff my way through that one.

"What sign?" I asked.

"You mean you don't remember?" he said — and I could hear his face fall. "I wrote to you about a year ago and told you I'd been to London and I'd stood across the street from your bookshop, watching the Marks & Co. sign swing in the breeze and thinking: 'I should steal that for Helene.' And you wrote back: 'Why didn't you?' "

On his return trip to London the next summer, he had gone to the London City Council and gotten permission to remove the sign; he'd found a London firm to crate it and ship it to his home in Nebraska; he was coming to New York on business in December and would deliver it to me personally in time for Christmas.

Three friends were on hand when Dan Kelly arrived with the unopened crate. I sat cross-legged on the carpet and pried the nails out, one by one. When the lid was finally removed, I lifted out of the crate two thin sheets of glass. Between them, on black cloth backing, large silver letters spelled out the legend:

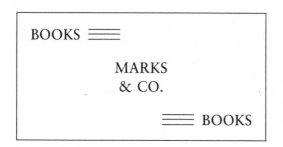

Few moments in my life have equalled that one. The three friends carted off the sign to have it framed for me and on Christmas Eve helped me hang it on the short alcove wall, at a right angle to the long wall of bookshelves holding all the books that came from there.

A few nights later, I was sitting over coffee after dinner, feasting my eyes on the sign. Flush with the base of it, on the bottom bookshelf, was a small row of books. They hadn't come from Marks & Co. Their cheap cloth covers were badly faded and I never read the books anymore. But year after year, when I tried to throw them out, they stubbornly refused to depart. I stared at the faded covers that hid the underlinings, the brackets, the margin notes with which one earnest, inadequate student had disfigured the seven volumes of Cambridge lectures by Sir Arthur Quiller-Couch. The time had come to add up what I owed to Q.

I owed him whatever literary education I had — and enough training in the craft of writing to have kept myself alive by it through the Sixties. I owed him my shelves full of books — and my choice of Marks & Co. over the column of New York bookstores. Wherefore I owed him *84, Charing Cross Road,* and *The Duchess of Bloomsbury Street* — and the hundreds if not thousands of friends both books had brought me in the mail and over the phone.

It was an awesome legacy for a Cambridge don to have conferred on a lowly pupil he never knew existed three thousand miles away.

I didn't know that all of it was only the legacy-so-far. The rest of it was waiting to be delivered to me, piecemeal, over the next several years, in London.

⇛ THREE ⇚

Drowning on Television

On a January day in 1975, a cable arrived in my agent's office and she called to read it to me.

KEEN TO ACQUIRE 84 CHARING CROSS ROAD
FOR BBC TELEVISION

MARK SHIVAS

Mark Shivas, she told me, was one of the BBC's best young producers. Being a fan of BBC television, I was very flattered. I phoned the news to all my friends and it was my friend Susan who said brightly:

"You'll see your whole life pass before you and you won't even have to drown."

In February, Hugh Whitemore's script arrived. I'd wondered how on earth he was going to turn a book of letters into television dialogue. He hadn't tried to. You might say he scorned to try. He'd let the letters themselves take the place of dialogue by doing the whole script in a television technique known as "voice-over."

"Voice-over" meant that the audience would hear a letter read by a disembodied voice while the owner of the voice performed pantomime action on the screen. To do an hour-long TV show this way from beginning to end required the kind of audacity known as "chutzpah."

A week later I got the news that Anne Jackson had been signed to play me, and Frank Finlay, a London stage star, would be playing Frank Doel. Then a letter arrived from Mark Shivas to say rehearsals would begin early in April and the show would be taped on April 25, 26, and 27. Was I coming over for it?

I had no work in the typewriter. I can only write about what happens to me and nothing much had happened to me lately. But it occurred to me that sitting in a TV studio watching an actress pretend to be me definitely classified as something-happening-to-me that I could write about afterward. I typed a few pages that were something between a memo and an outline and sent it to the *Reader's Digest*. And the *Digest* — a Lord Bountiful among magazines — agreed to stake me to a ten-day trip to London for the last week of rehearsals and the three days of taping provided I was willing to travel economy-style.

"We presume she doesn't have to stay at the Dorchester?" was the way the *Digest* editor put it to my agent. Who answered promptly: "No, no. Cheap-cheap."

"Cheap-cheap" was the slogan of BOAC's Show Tours that season. The next day I went down to the BOAC office on Fifth Avenue and bought a Show Tour ticket. The package included a hotel room on Russell Square — and where would I rather wake up on an April morning?

Then one night I saw Anne Jackson and her husband, Eli Wallach, on a TV talk show. They were obviously warm, friendly people and the thought of what I was planning to do to one of them appalled me. Maxine, the bosom friend of my youth, was an actress and I tried to imagine the look on her dramatic face if she had to rehearse the part of a real woman and found the real woman sitting in the rehearsal room staring at her while she did it. I worried about this for a few days. Then the BBC phone calls started coming and I forgot about Anne Jackson.

I'd always marveled at the absolute authenticity of BBC productions. I was to spend the next few weeks in New York and London finding out how they achieved it, and my education began with those phone calls.

The first call came early one morning. I said hello and a woman at the other end shouted over a bad connection that she was calling from London, her name was Beryl and she was assistant to Mark Cullingham, the director of "84, Charing Cross Road."

"We'd so much appreciate it if you'd take the following books down to the BBC office in Rockefeller Center to be mailed to us, to be used in the production," she said. "Have you a pencil?"

And she named eight of my oldest and most cherished books. She might as well have said, "We'd so much like you to mail us eight of your fingers."

Fortunately, I had an excuse.

"You couldn't possibly use them on camera," I said. "They've been on open bookshelves by a window for twenty years — and between air pollution and steam heat, they're all wrecks! The covers are cracked, some of the bindings have edges so ragged you'd think mice had chewed them."

"Not to worry!" Beryl shouted firmly across three thousand miles of ocean static. "If you can take them down tomorrow in time for the four o'clock mail pouch we'd-be-so-grateful."

Anybody but a congenital worm would have said "No!" But I stood at the phone meekly writing down the address of the BBC office and agreeing to deliver the books in the morning.

I got them down from the shelves and looked at them and my heart failed. The green leather cover of my *Elizabethan Poets* — a present from all my friends in the bookshop — was faded and cracked at the edges, but at least the cover was still firmly attached. The cover of Newman's *Idea of a University,* with its dusty gold seal, was so loose I didn't think it would survive the trip. But the next morning I took them all down to the BBC office and handed them over to a stranger with all the confidence of a mother handing over her sickly infant to be shipped across the ocean without her.

A few days later Beryl phoned again.

"Do you still have the luncheon cloth sent you by the bookshop for Christmas in 1953?" she inquired.

I don't know what I answered to that one but it was something noncommittal: "I'm not sure," or "I'll have to look." Whatever it was, Beryl translated as Yes.

"Well, *would* you take it down to the BBC office to be mailed to us?" she said briskly. "We'll take very good care of it."

The cloth, which had been embroidered by old Mrs. Boulton, Frank Doel's neighbor, was round. Since I'd bought an oblong dinner table when I moved into my palace, I'd finally given the cloth to my friends Kay and Brian Huson — less because they had a round Colonial table than because Brian, an Englishman, had known all about my correspondence with Marks & Co. In the days when I worried because I could afford to send only one parcel for the entire shop, it was Brian who had assured me that the Charing Cross Road bookshops were "all quite small."

I had a hunch the cloth was still in their house in Ro-wayton, Connecticut. Unfortunately, Kay and Brian weren't. They were in Beirut, where Brian was working for an American bank. Their two sons would be no help since both were at Brian's old school in England. On the chance that there were tenants in the house I phoned the Connecticut number.

A woman answered and said Yes, she and her husband were the Husons' tenants but she'd never met them. Her husband, a British civil servant, had met Brian in Beirut and rented the house from him there. Understandably, she wasn't about to rummage through Kay's linens for me, but she said she'd discuss the problem with her husband and call me back.

She phoned the next morning to say that her husband had talked to the Husons in Beirut (they sent their love) and she'd found the cloth and was mailing it to me. It arrived and I took it down to the BBC. And Beryl made her third and last call.

"Do you have photographs of your old flat and your present flat?" she asked. I said I had no photos of either and Beryl said:

"Well, *would* you have some taken of your present flat and mail them to us? The designer is most anxious to have them."

So that evening an obliging gent who lived on the sixteenth floor came down to my eighth-floor apartment carrying his Christmas camera with the long lens, and photographed every inch of the living room and alcove. A few days later, a set of glossy color prints went off by airmail to London.

Late in March, Anne Jackson phoned.

"I'm leaving for London next week to start rehearsals for '84, Charing Cross Road,' " she said. "Can I come around and meet you before I go?"

Feeling very English, we made a date for her to come to tea at four the following Friday. ("*Just* tea," she said firmly. "I'm dieting.") At exactly four on Friday my doorbell rang and I opened the door to her. Annie — which I was told to call her before she'd been here two minutes — was startlingly beautiful. She had perfect cameo features, a flawless milky complexion and a thick mass of burnished red hair. Having been plain and mousy all my life, I thought: "What a face to be playing me!" But we were the same height, we both wore sweaters, pants and flat-heeled shoes, and Annie got so carried away by this she announced:

"We look alike!"

"Don't I wish it," I said.

She walked in and headed straight for the bookshelves, which won my heart. Few visitors do that.

Over tea, we discovered we both came from Pennsylvania, we both had half-blind left eyes and we shared a couple of other ten-cent characteristics I've forgotten but which seemed of heavy significance at the time. By the third cup of tea we were such old friends I said:

"Please tell me honestly" — which is what you say when you want to force a kind soul to lie — "If I come over for the last week of rehearsal, will it bother you to have me there?"

"Of course not!" said Annie gallantly. "You have to come!"

She told me she'd be staying at Brian Aherne's house in Maida Vale.

"They're living in Switzerland and they've lent me the house for a month. But I'm taking my sister, Bea, along for company, and during the last week Eli and our son Peter will be there. So I can't offer to put you up. But I want you to come to Maida Vale every evening you have nothing to do. I don't want you sitting alone in a hotel room."

She gave me Brian Aherne's address and wrote the name of my hotel in her pocket address book. Then she got out a tape recorder and had me read a few of the *84* letters into it so she could study my voice. When she left I felt as if I'd known her for years.

Two long newsy letters came from Brian Aherne's house in the next two weeks. Annie reported that every member of the cast had gone alone into a soundproof room to record his or her letters on tape; that Frank Finlay was a wonderful actor to work with; and that Mark Shivas was a love. A third week crawled by, and I was finally on my way back to London.

It was too early for the roses in Russell Square, but when I walked into the hotel room, there was a water glass full of pink garden roses on the dresser. Propped against the glass was a note:

Picked this morning and covered with greenfly. Welcome!

Mark Shivas

Alongside it were two messages. One said that a BBC car would call for me at nine the next morning to drive me to the BBC Rehearsal Block in North Acton. The other said that Miss Anne Jackson expected me for dinner the following evening.

At nine the next morning the desk phoned to say the BBC car was waiting, and I went down to the lobby. The desk clerk pointed out a slight young man waiting by the door and when I reached him he said:

"Miss Hanff? I'm your driver."

"Isn't it a beautiful day?" I said. The driver hesitated a moment. Then he said:

"I'm also your producer. Mark Shivas" — and stuck out a hand.

Everything about Shivas was unassuming, including the battered green jalopy he helped me into. I told him it wasn't the limousine I'd planned to become accustomed to, and he said No, it was a colorful, democratic car that liked Americans. The jalopy coughed its way out onto a highway and I asked:

"How far is it to North Acton?"

"Forty-five minutes," said Shivas. "Less, of course, in a fine car like mine."

We talked about London neighborhoods — he told me he lived down in the East End, across the river — and then I said:

"All my life I've wanted to meet a producer so I could ask him this. What exactly does a producer do?"

"A producer," said Shivas, "finds a book he likes, and picks the best adapter for it — and the best director — and the best cast — and the best set designer. Then he sits back and lets everybody else do the work."

"But you oversee rehearsals," I said.

"Oh, no," said Mark. "I never go to rehearsals. I keep out of the way till the taping starts."

Translation:

He lived in the East End, at the other end of town from Russell Square in Bloomsbury. He had no reason to be at that morning's rehearsal and wouldn't stay for it. He had driven through London's morning rush-hour traffic to get

me, and was now driving all the way out to North Acton —
where he would turn around and drive back to his London
office — just so I wouldn't have to make the trip with an
impersonal BBC driver on my first day and wouldn't have
to introduce myself when I got there.

I asked what shows he'd produced and he said his first
show was "The Six Wives of Henry VIII." It was several
years in the past and I said:

"You don't look old enough to have produced that."
And he told me he'd been the youngest producer the BBC
had ever hired when they trusted him with it. (He's produced a string of prize-winning TV shows since then, including my favorite "Glittering Prizes," and it's typical of
Mark Shivas that all his productions are famous while he
stays unobtrusively in the background.)

The BBC Rehearsal Block is a seven-story building that's
permanently unfurnished. There's a cafeteria on the top
floor but the other floors have only large, empty rehearsal
rooms. When a cast is rehearsing in one of them, a few
pieces of prop furniture are installed. They're removed when
rehearsals end.

The cast of "84" was rehearsing when we walked in.
But Annie, sitting at an old typewriter table at the far end
of the room, saw me and rose, and she and I loped toward
each other, met in the middle of the room and embraced,
murmuring reassuring nothings to each other. That stopped
rehearsal for a few minutes and Mark introduced me to
the rest of the cast and to Mark Cullingham, the director.
Then he left for London, I retired to one of the folding
chairs along a side wall and rehearsal resumed.

At one end of the room was the makeshift bookshop
set: two desks, a few straight chairs and an old bookshelf.
At the other end, Annie presided over a studio couch, a

typewriter table and an ancient kitchen stove. There were books on the typewriter table but they weren't mine. The books in the bookshop set weren't mine either. The cast was rehearsing with prop books and I wondered where mine were. Then I forgot them and concentrated on the rehearsal.

Somebody turned on a tape recorder, I heard Annie's voice begin a letter to Frank Doel — and Annie began to perform the pantomime action of dressing to go out. Her action had to be timed to the split second so that, after buttoning a blouse, putting on a sweater, picking up a handbag and a manuscript, she went out the door at the precise instant when her taped voice ended the letter. Frank Finlay and the others in the bookshop set had to time their action just as precisely, but their scenes had bits of dialogue, which gave them a respite now and then. Annie worked alone and got no respite at all.

During the lunch break, Frank Finlay told me he was taking Nora Doel and her daughters to supper after his performance that night. He was starring in a West End play, acting every night and rehearsing in "84" all day, and he was giving Nora, Sheila and Mary tickets to the show and taking them to supper afterward because that was the only free time he had, to ask them questions about Frank Doel.

When rehearsal ended, Mark Cullingham introduced me to the set designer, who showed me the model of the bookshop set and asked me about the layout of my 95th Street apartment. By the time I got back to Russell Square it was too late to walk around Bloomsbury. There was barely time to dress for dinner at Annie's.

If you're old enough to have seen Brian Aherne on stage

in *The Barretts of Wimpole Street* or in a whole string of Hollywood comedies back in the Thirties and Forties, you'll know why it seemed very glamorous to me to be on my way to his house. It was one of a row of grandly Victorian houses on the street where the Regent's Park canal ends. The canal-boat passengers were stepping ashore a few yards up the street as I got out of a cab.

I went up the broad front steps and rang the doorbell and Annie came to the door. She dragged me along a hall and then down a steep flight of steps to the kitchen — and opened the oven door with a flourish, to show me what she'd done for me. In the oven, alongside a sizzling roast, was a Yorkshire pudding she'd made from the recipe in "84" which she'd been rehearsing in pantomime for two weeks.

Beautiful as the house was, I could understand why the Ahernes didn't live in it. Victorian London houses were built for "Upstairs, Downstairs" families with plenty of servants, and the servants were of no concern at all to the architect. So when dinner was ready, Annie and her sister, Bea, had to carry heavy dinner platters of roast beef, Yorkshire pudding and vegetables up two steep flights of steps to the dining room. (I was only trusted with the bread tray and coffee pot.)

We adjourned for coffee to a dramatically beautiful drawing room. The walls were covered in deep brown velvet, set off by a great white stone fireplace and gleaming white woodwork; and the matching brown velvet sofa where we curled up with our coffee faced a long window wall of nubby white silk drapes.

It was the first of several relaxed and chatty evenings I spent there and those evenings gave Annie and me a grin months later when we discovered we'd both been working during them. Annie'd been studying me for the next day's rehearsal; I'd been studying her for the *Digest* article.

(How much she'd learned about me in those evenings I didn't discover till a year later. Watching her at rehearsals, I was aware of one characteristic she'd caught. Like all very nearsighted people, I'm awkward and clumsy. Annie had seen this in my attempts to help her in Brian Aherne's kitchen: what I didn't spill I dropped. In her pantomime, she not only caught this clumsiness and made it funny, she somehow made it appealing. But a year later, when "84" was shown on PBS, a friend told me: "Her gestures were so like yours it was spooky!" And another friend phoned from California to say: "I know you recorded the letters yourself. I recognized your voice.")

I met Nora and Sheila Doel one night for dinner, and they were full of their evening with Frank Finlay.

"He questioned us for two hours, Helen," said Nora. (She never did learn to call me Helene.) "He wanted to know about Frank's gestures and his mannerisms and what clothes he liked. He made Sheila get up and show him how Frank walked, and she walked back and forth for him and he watched her. Then he got up and tried it — and he walked so like my Frank I couldn't look."

Rehearsals ended on a Thursday; on Friday, the production was to move to the BBC Television Center at Shepherd's Bush for the three days of taping. On Thursday afternoon, when the last run-through ended, Mark Cullingham took my arm and escorted me ceremoniously to the long table at the back of the room where the set models had stood. There, set out in two neat rows, were my books. I stared at them and I couldn't speak. They had been transformed.

What I was staring at in light-headed disbelief was a row of leather covers that had for years had ragged, chewed-looking edges. The original covers were still there, but they were miraculously whole again. Which was only part of the transformation. The once-faded green leather binding of my *Elizabethan Poets* was clear emerald, its gold-tipped pages gleamed, its chewed edges were gone. The cover of my Newman was firmly attached, its deep brown pigskin glowed with a patina it had never had in my lifetime, and the long-faded gold seal shone against it. On all the books, old stains were gone, imbedded dust was gone, the covers were fresh and bright again.

"We called Buckingham Palace and got the name of the Queen's bookbinder, and he restored them for us," I heard Mark Cullingham say. "The leather's heated till it's pliable and then it's stretched downward and the ragged edges are cut off." He went on talking about the special solution for cleaning the gold and I still couldn't speak. I don't know how long it was before I managed to thank somebody.

The schedule for the BBC's three-day taping of "84" would have caused riots in any other industry: 10 a.m. to 10 p.m., Friday, Saturday and Sunday. At 9 a.m. on Friday, Mark Shivas called for me in the jalopy and we drove out to Shepherd's Bush. And it's too bad the BBC TV Production Center isn't open to tourists. The building is astonishing and, as far as I know, unique.

It's a grey-and-green stone oval, several stories high, with no windows and only one door. Inside the door, whether you turn left or right, if you keep walking long enough you'll eventually come around to the door again. But you don't go left or right, you walk straight ahead, across the lobby and through a pair of swinging doors. As Mark pushed them open he said blandly:

"The show's being taped in 'Studio 6 of the Green Assembly.' "

Then he pointed upward, at the ceiling.

Strung along wires under the ceiling were three crisscrossing strings of small lights, like Christmas tree lights, one set red, one green, one blue, each set branching off in a separate direction. We followed the green lights, but as we went along corridors and down steps and through more corridors and up steps, the green lights crisscrossed the red lights at one turn and the blue ones at another, so constantly that a stranger could get hopelessly lost. The building is a maze.

We came to a large green neon sign reading STUDIO 1 and walked past four more signs till we came to Studio 6. There, Mark pointed my way down the Dressing Rooms corridor. Then he left me and I followed more green lights and signs, past Dressing Rooms 18, 19 and 20, and came to Dressing Room 21, where Kate Binchy, the pretty Irish actress who was playing Nora Doel, wanted me to see her 1950s wardrobe and the silver-framed wedding photograph she and Frank Finlay had posed for, to be used in the Doels' living-room set. Ten minutes after I got there, Chris, the floor-manager (equivalent to a theatre stage-manager), came for me and took me out to the studio floor.

"I want you to see your bookshop," he said.

The studio floor was a vast clearing in an encircling forest of wires and cables that rose from floor to ceiling, completely hiding the walls. Spaced across the floor were the three sets to be used in that day's taping: my former apartment, the Doels' living room and the one large set which would be in use on all three days: the bookshop. It was walled off from our view as we approached it.

"The two Marks and the set designer," Chris told me

as we walked, "went to all the secondhand bookshops in London to talk to people who had once worked at Marks & Co. They quizzed them about where every desk and door and staircase had been. Then the designer went home and drew a sketch of the shop and took it back to them for correction till he'd got every detail right. So," he finished, "what you'll see is an exact replica of your bookshop, reduced to scale."

And he walked me around to the bookshop's glass front door and opened it for me and I walked into my bookshop. It was shabby and comfortable, with old desks and lamps and a solid old staircase. The bookshelves were exactly as my friend Maxine had described them to me in a letter — heavy oak that had turned grey with "must and dust and age." I gravitated to the shelves and found them crammed with books. Not the usual stage "prop" books — dilapidated junkshop volumes collected at random to fill up the shelves. The books on these shelves were those of a genuine antiquarian bookshop, many with fine bindings, some just old, with the musty smell of buried treasure.

"They were all lent to us by London booksellers," Chris said. "They feel a proprietary interest in the show."

He left me and I started to browse among the books. I was still at it when Mark came for me at ten, and led the way up a ladder to the glass-enclosed control booth.

Most of the booth was taken up by a half-moon table brightly lit by five studio lamps, one at each of the stations identified by placards: Producer, Director, Assistant to the Director, Vision Mixer, Lighting Director. The two Marks found an extra chair and made room between them at the table for me and my notebook and pencils.

When I looked straight ahead, I saw five monitors suspended in a black void. When I leaned over and looked down, I saw the studio floor so far below that the sets looked like three doll houses flung far apart across a wooden plain, surrounded by a towering wire jungle.

Chris, in charge of floor operations, was already getting instructions over his walkie-talkie from Mark Cullingham, who spoke into a table mike. It was Mark Cullingham's stream of instructions, to be relayed by Chris to members of the cast, that told me why it took three twelve-hour days to tape a one-hour TV show.

Television has no equivalent of a stage dress rehearsal. In the theatre, dress rehearsals take place on the stage of the theatre where the play is to open. They may go on for a week or more, all day long and sometimes far into the night. But the cast and crew of a TV show have the use of a studio only on the three days of taping, which means that every scene has to be dress-rehearsed on the studio floor on the day it's to be taped. And since visual effects are of first importance to the camera, every scene has to be dress-rehearsed over and over until every visual detail is perfect. So Mark Cullingham's instructions to Chris were a steady stream of hair-splitting corrections:

"Has that door been moved or is John not on his marks?"

"Ask Frank to tip his head a bit more to the right. . . . Yes, and can he lower his hand with the letter in it so we see his face? . . . No, that's too low. . . . That's good. All right, once more, please."

And since the director oversees every detail with God-like authority, any small deviation from rehearsed movements is sacrilege.

"Annie's gone completely mad! She looked at her watch! She's never done that before! . . . All right, once more, please."

"Once more, please" was a mechanical refrain, like a dentist's "Open wide, please," as every scene was rehearsed and rehearsed five or six times — though each scene contained only one letter or two and ran only a couple of minutes. Not until Mark Cullingham had pinpointed and corrected every microscopic visual flaw did he say into the mike:

"All right, let's go for a recording."

And Chris's youthful voice would rise to an authoritative bellow:

"All right! Vairry q-u-a-a-t, please! This is a recording! VAIRRY VAIRRY Q-U-A-A-T!"

And the scene was videotaped. Then dress rehearsals began on the next two-minute scene.

I spent the morning thinking that if I were Annie or Frank Finlay it would drive me crazy to be constantly nagged about the angle of my head or the position of my hand when I was trying to concentrate on acting. But when we adjourned to the top-floor cafeteria for lunch, I mentioned this to Annie and she looked faintly surprised and said, Oh, no, that was no problem. And Kate Binchy, overhearing this, explained it in a single sentence:

"All the interior work's been done."

Through three weeks of rehearsal, the cast's and the director's only concern had been with what each character was thinking and feeling. So by the day the taping began, Annie and Frank and the rest of the cast had their interpretations locked inside their heads where the incessant visual instructions couldn't touch them.

I was so fascinated by the technical details of the videotaping and so busy getting it all down in my notebook I was only vaguely aware that the words being spoken were from the letters in *84, Charing Cross Road.* We were having dinner on the cafeteria's outdoor porch when somebody asked me:

"How does it feel to see yourself on television?"

I wasn't seeing myself on television. I was seeing Annie Jackson, moving around in an English bed-sitter that bore no resemblance whatsoever to my old converted apartment.

That was on Friday. On Saturday — I suppose because I'd got used to the videotaping process by then and could ignore it — something inside me began to change. As gradually as stepping from very shallow water into slightly deeper water, I began to see the bookshop set, not as a set, but as my bookshop. Frank Finlay, looking more and more like the snapshots of Frank Doel Nora had sent me, spoke the letters in a voice, and with inflections, so exactly as I'd imagined Frank Doel to sound when I'd read his letters that the two Franks became one. And when Frank picked up a book that was unmistakably mine and handed it to one of the girls to mail to me, the illusion was overpowering: Frank Doel was still alive, the other friends I'd made in the bookshop still worked there, the shop itself was still thriving at 84, Charing Cross Road.

Late that afternoon, as I was watching the bookshop staff open one of the Christmas parcels, remembering Brian Huson's "the bookshops are all quite small," a messenger tiptoed into the control booth and laid a slip of paper in my lap with a single sentence on it:

Mr. Brian Huson will pick you up for dinner at six in the lobby.

The explanation was as matter-of-fact as the very British Mr. Huson himself. (English doesn't describe him; he's British, like the Empire.)

"I'm staying at my club. I flew in from Beirut yesterday on business," he said as we drove to a nearby restaurant. "After dinner last night I was in the lounge looking through a copy of *Radio Times* and I came on a story about '84, Charing Cross Road' being filmed this weekend. So this morning I phoned the BBC and they said Yes, you were here and you had an hour's dinner break at six."

We lingered over dinner so I was late getting back to the control booth. As I slid into my seat at the half-moon table and looked out at the central monitor, I saw old Mrs. Boulton working on the Husons' luncheon cloth.

At ten p.m. when the taping ended and we drove back to London, I was vaguely depressed. I told myself I was tired; it had been a long two days of note-taking.

But that night I dreamed of the bookshop. I'd never dreamed about it before but I'd never had a concrete picture of it in my mind before. Now I saw it vividly. I saw Frank and the girls and Bill Humphries and Mr. Marks, the owner. They were all busy dusting the bookshelves and straightening the books, and Frank was putting a tumbler of pink garden roses on his desk — all because I was finally coming to London and they were getting ready to welcome me. Then it was a sunny morning, I was stepping out of a car onto the sidewalk of Charing Cross Road and walking up to the bookshop door. But the shop was closed. Its empty windows were dirty and the letters over the glass door were chipped and peeling. I tried the door and it swung open and I walked into a cold, bare room with dismantled bookshelves lying on the floor, and an empty staircase running up to rooms I knew were as desolate and abandoned as the one I stood in.

The dream woke me. And lying there in the darkness at two or three in the morning, I tried not to hear the lines that were like a dirge in my head:

> *"Tell them I came, and no one answered,*
> *That I kept my word," he said. . . .*

I fell asleep eventually. I woke Sunday morning to bright sunshine and it was easy to put the bad dream out of my mind and enjoy the day's taping.

Since it was my last night, I had dinner with my only close friends in London, Leo and Ena Marks, son and daughter-in-law of Marks & Co. We'd seen so little of each other in the ten days I'd been there that we sat a long time over dinner and I was an hour late getting back to the control booth. If I'd gone back earlier, I'd have watched half a dozen rehearsals of the scene in progress, which would have lessened the impact. As it was, I slid into my seat just as Chris was calling for quiet. A moment later I saw, coming up on the screen in front of me, my own apartment. I saw my slatted coffee-table and beyond it, the grey drapes at the picture window. I was vaguely aware that the desk wasn't mine and that the bookshelves were on the wrong wall. Then Annie walked into the room. She had mail in her hand. She opened a letter and stood reading it — while the impersonal voice of a secretary told her Frank Doel was dead. I sat remembering the January night when I'd come home from the library to find that wrong-looking letter waiting for me. And when Annie, in a moving gesture, swept up a load of books in her arms, my throat tightened and I looked away from the monitor for a minute.

When I looked back, Annie was curled up on the floor, sorting books. My books.

I was looking at my own apartment and at books that were unmistakably mine, but I wasn't there. Somebody else was going through my books. Suddenly, it was a visible fact to me that Frank Doel wasn't the only one who had died. I must have died, too — or how could someone else be sitting on the floor a few feet from my coffee-table, pawing through my most cherished books as if they were hers? When she picked up *Elizabethan Poets*, the green cover itself seemed to cry out to me for rescue. I wanted to shout:

"Put that down, it's mine! It was a present from the shop — from Frank and everybody!"

I didn't shout. Like the dead heroine of *Our Town* watching the living move about in her childhood home, I knew my shout wouldn't be heard. But she had been seeing the past. I was looking at the future and I was powerless to prevent it. I didn't know I was crying, till Beryl reached across Mark Cullingham to press my hand firmly and whisper: "Are you all right?" (meaning Pull yourself together). And I sobbed testily:

"Of course I'm not all right! Anybody can see I'm a complete mess!" And Shivas laughed and put an arm around me, and I swam up from the dark waters and back to the land of the living.

A year later the show was bought by PBS and I finally got to see it. There was a special preview showing at Channel 13, for me "and seventy-five close friends" — meaning my six close friends and the entire Democratic Club — and I was nervously wondering whether I was going to start weeping again, at the sight of the bookshop I'd waited too long to visit or the preview of my own Passing. But I didn't weep. I watched the screening with unalloyed pleasure. On the night of the broadcast I watched it a second time on my best friend's color TV set with even more pleasure. I loved it from beginning to end and I could have watched it a dozen more times if I'd been let.

You only drown once.

FOUR

Fan Fare

PROLOGUE

IN 1975 THERE WERE no longer any shoeboxes of fan mail on my closet shelf; they'd been gone for over a year. What happened was that after *The Duchess* came out in both countries I'd acquired several more shoeboxes full of mail till the stack of them reached nearly to the hanging light bulb. And one night as I opened the closet door and pulled the light cord, the bulb burned out in a momentary flash of blue flame — an inch or two from the shoeboxes. The closet is just inside the front door; the only other exit in case of fire is out the eighth-floor window.

I replaced the light bulb. But when I went to bed that night I couldn't fall asleep. I kept seeing those shoeboxes jammed with dried paper an inch or two from the little blue flame. Finally I got out of bed, carried the armload of shoeboxes down the hall and sadly dropped down the incinerator a couple of thousand beautiful testimonials to my talent and character. From then on I threw away every fan letter as soon as I answered it — except for one special handful.

Each year a few letters came in from English readers who wanted to show me the literary sights in their home towns. These letters I stashed in the England Corner — a back corner of the breakfront where I kept my passport, London address book and the maps of London and England we all know I couldn't read. Now and then on a winter evening, I'd take them out and reread them, and throw away those too old to make use of if I ever did get to England for a literary sightseeing tour. I remember one, for instance, from an Oxford don, offering to show me Newman's rooms at Oriel. "But don't wait too long," he warned. "I'm eighty-four." Rereading it three years later, in the summer of '77, I threw it away; I'd waited too long. For a grim economic reason.

Between 1974 and 1977, I managed the considerable feat of writing three successive books which had to go down the incinerator. A fourth, written on commission — a tourist guide to New York called *Apple of My Eye* — was published, but the money I got for it just paid my living expenses while I researched and wrote it. I wasn't earning enough in royalties to afford another trip to England, and in the fall of '77, in a fit of housecleaning and pessimism, I threw away the clutch of fan letters still in the England Corner.

But that winter, a few more dribbled in.

Dear Miss Hanff,

. . . If you come to Winchester, we'd love to show you Izaak Walton's memorial and Jane Austen's grave in Winchester Cathedral. And afterwards, we'd drive you the short distance to Chawton to see Jane's house.

I must warn you, we are a retired couple and very dull.

Jean Gomme

Dear Miss Hanff,

I am a friend of the caretaker of John Henry Newman's house at Littlemore. If you come again to Oxford, I could arrange to have you taken through the house. . . .

Dear Miss Hanff,

I am one of those umbrella-waving tourist guides you avoided when you toured London. I'm so sorry you never got to the Tower of London while you were here.

If you ever come again, I'd love to give you a personally guided tour of the Tower, and show you some things you missed at Westminster Abbey.

I promise not to bring the umbrella no matter how hard it's raining.

Judy Summers

There was a letter from a girl named Doris, who worked in a Brighton bookshop and wanted to show me the Pavilion "if you can come on a Sunday."

Then one morning my phone rang and a light, rather husky English voice that could have been male or female said:

"Miss Hanff? I've just finished reading *Apple of My Eye* and I loved it. I love New York, I come over every year."

"Where are you staying?" I asked.

"Oh, I'm not there now," said the voice. "I'm calling from London."

"What part of London?" I asked. There was a pause.

"Well, actually," said the voice, "I'm calling from Harrow School infirmary. I have the flu."

I said I didn't think his parents would appreciate the long-distance phone call and he said:

"Oh, my mother won't mind, she calls New York all the time, she loves it, too."

He asked what other books I'd written. I gave him the titles and wished him a speedy recovery, and we hung up. A week later, the letter arrived:

Dear Miss Hanff,

I am the fifteen-year-old Harrow schoolboy who phoned you last week. I have just read The Duchess of Bloomsbury Street and I enjoyed it very much but I have one criticism.

You spent three full pages on Eton, and you never even mentioned Harrow. Why don't you come back to London next summer? You could stay with my mother and me at our house in Kensington and my mother would drive us to Harrow and I would give you the Grand Tour.

Peter Astaire

Then in March the bone-crusher arrived.

Dear Miss Hanff,

I am the widow of Frederic Brittain, biographer of Sir Arthur Quiller-Couch. . . .

If you ever come to Cambridge I'll give you tea in Q's rooms and biscuits from his tobacco jar.

Muriel Brittain

I got down my copy of the Brittain biography and saw that it had been published in 1948. I wondered how old Muriel Brittain was.

"Don't wait too long."

I got out my maps and saw (or decided) that all the places fans wanted me to visit were within a day's round trip of London. I could manage the plane fare, but a Show Tour package would give me too little time, and the cost of a hotel room and three restaurant meals a day would break the bank entirely. I stewed about this for a week or two. Then one fine April morning André Deutsch came to breakfast.

André is a London publisher with a special fondness for American authors. He's the English publisher of John Updike, John Kenneth Galbraith, Peter Benchley and Marilyn French, just to name those I can remember offhand. And every year he comes to New York to buy new books for his list and see all his American authors, including me. The phone will ring one morning and a Continental voice will announce:

"Helene? Darling, it's André, I just got in from London. Can you give me breakfast on Tuesday? At eight o'clock?"

Or he forgets to phone and comes anyway. I assume he makes up a tentative schedule on the plane coming over because one year, on a hot July morning, I was in the kitchen getting breakfast in my bra and bikini panties when the buzzer sounded and the doorman said into the intercom:

"Gentleman on the way up."

It was 7:50 by the kitchen clock and I said:

"What-do-you-mean, a gentleman on the way up at this hour! Who is he?"

The doorman asked the caller's name and reported:

"Mr. Deutsch."

I hadn't known he was in town. I tore into the living room — which hadn't been dusted lately — and barely made it inside a T-shirt and slacks when André walked in. He kissed me and I said:

"You might have let me know you were coming!"

And André said reasonably:

"I must have, darling. It's down in my book." And he showed me his pocket engagement book where it said under Tuesday, "8 a.m. Breakfast with Helene."

I love him, so it didn't matter. I love him for many reasons but especially because he's not a faceless corporation on three floors of a skyscraper, he's a man — slight, grey-haired, with a thin tanned face, an exotic accent (he was born in Hungary) and a very dapper wardrobe.

That April morning over our bacon and eggs I told him about the literary sights fans wanted to show me.

"I've got the fare and enough money for incidental expenses," I said. "What I need is a free flat for a few weeks."

"You can have my house!" said André, pleased. "I'm going to China and India for a month, I leave on twenty-first July." And he added: "Workmen will be there. I'm having a new story added onto the house. But they'll be up on the roof, they won't bother you."

Anyone who's ever had workmen building an extra floor to the house will find that sentence hilarious. But André and I were innocents and the plan seemed perfectly feasible to us. He described the house enthusiastically, gave me the address and telephone number and told me to land at Heathrow during office hours so his secretary could meet the plane and drive me to the house and turn over the keys to me.

As soon as he left, I got out my map and located the street he lived on. It was either in Chelsea or South Kensington (the map was a little vague) but it was unmistakably down below Buckingham Palace. I don't like it down there.

My London begins up at Regent's Park and runs through Marylebone and Bloomsbury, Mayfair and Soho, on its way down to the Mall where it ends at St. James's Park and Green Park. Everything below that, I regard as No Man's Land. But I rose above the fact that André lived in the wrong part of town and phoned my friends to announce that I had a London town house for three summer weeks.

That night I dashed off a letter to Ena Marks asking if she and Leo would like to spend a couple of August weeks driving hither and yon to meet my fans and see the literary sights they wanted to show me. Back came a cable: IT'S A DATE LETTER FOLLOWS ALL OUR LOVE ENA AND LEO.

I went down to British Airways and bought my ticket and then I wrote to the fans involved, giving them my arrival and departure dates and André's address.

A letter arrived from Ena, suggesting I send her a list of the fans' names and addresses so she could get in touch with them and start making up a touring schedule.

"I have several painting commissions but I'm hoping to finish them by the time you come," she wrote. (Ena's a portrait painter, under her maiden name, Elena Gaussen.) "Marcus the cat sends love. As for Leo, well, he is still making sorties to this planet when he can spare the time from whichever part of outer space he comes from.

Your loving Ena"

I mailed her the list and asked her to keep my first week free for London fans, and to add Ayot St. Lawrence to the list of tours just because I was panting to see it. The only other person I wrote to was Abbe.

Abbe had entered my life — for ten minutes — back in June of '71. A fan letter arrived from a young woman who said she'd just graduated from college and had been given 84 as a graduation present. The letter was funny. (She had graduated from Hunter College, which she spelled gravely "Huntah," giving it the Brooklyn pronunciation.) But what intrigued me most was the address. I could look out of my windows and see the apartment house she lived in, right across the street.

It was quicker to phone her than to write a thank-you note, so I called her and said:

"Why didn't you just hand the letter to the doorman?"

She said she hadn't wanted to be a nuisance — but since I mentioned it, could she leave her copy of the book with the doorman for me to autograph? I was on my lunch hour and I said:

"You can bring it over now if you want to."

Her letter had been witty and relaxed. But when she came, she was solemn, round-faced and bespectacled — and suddenly I was looking at Myself When Young: easy and assured on paper, awkward and stiff in person. She was hunting for a job in publishing and I phoned a couple of editors for her, but before they got around to seeing her Abbe called to tell me she had a job at CBS. I congratulated her and then forgot about her. One year later, in July of '72, she phoned to say she was going to London for two weeks, and I wished her Bon Voyage.

She never came home. Or say that she took one look at London and discovered she *was* home.

The first London letter arrived in September telling me she had gotten herself a job working backstage in a London theatre.

"I'm tea-girl," she wrote. "I make tea for forty people — cast and crew — in a huge vat down in the basement. I also mop the stage before every performance and I sew an actor's tights back together when they split which they've done several times on this show."

The theatre was paying her fifteen pounds a week and I didn't ask how she lived on it. I was writing *The Duchess* at the time and I used her as shamelessly as the theatre did. Abbe chased all over London for me, checking street addresses and bulletin-board notices and mews signs. She sent me the information in letters that jumped with the life of the "hotel" in St. Martin's Lane where she was living.

"It's really a rooming-house for theatricals run by ex-theatricals," she wrote. "The roof in my room leaks but it's not a big problem because when it rains, the manageress leaves a bucket in my room and the main leak is over the sink anyway."

"The walls are a bit thin, so when Derek, the man next door, starts snoring I just elbow the wall and he turns over. We've decided it's like being married only with a partition down the middle of the matrimonial bed. If I'm reading in bed and I laugh at something, he'll call:

" 'Oo, wot is it, luv?' and I have to shout the passage through the wall."

When I was in London for the TV show I phoned her, and it took the hotel operator five minutes to connect me. Then Abbe said, slightly breathless:

"There's only one phone, it's in the lobby, they shout up for us. I had to run down five flights is why it took so long."

During the three years since then, her letters had kept coming, though I don't think I answered one in four.

"My mother was here for Christmas. She took one look at my room and said: 'I lived better than this during the Depression.' Then she said: 'For two hundred years, immigrants have been coming to the United States to improve their living standard. YOU emigrate back to Europe to live in a tenement.' Now she pelts me with letters on the subject.

I am strongly considering writing *Deceased* on her next letter and returning it to sender."

Then came a letter announcing she'd landed a permanent job at a West End theatre working the lighting board as assistant to the electrician. From then on I got to know the backstage crew, especially Ron, the electrician, and Beerbohm Tree, the theatre cat.

"After Beerbohm caught three mice we told the manager he ought to be paid, as he was the theatre exterminator, and the manager agreed to pay for his cat food." Beerbohm got into a fight with another tomcat and needed an expensive trip to the vet for a bleeding eye, "So we put him on payroll for one matinee as B. Tree, duties unspecified."

The last letter I'd had reported that the St. Martin's hotel had closed and Abbe had moved into Sandringham Flats — "on Charing Cross Road of which you may have heard." The flats had no elevators, no bathtubs and no showers. But her fourth-floor walk-up had a balcony "and wonderful neighbors — mostly pub staff, writers, the Unemployed and ex-theatricals (a wig lady from films)." She didn't mind having no bathtub; she did mind having no phone.

"The phone company has heard a rumor that the building is to be torn down so they are arranging not to install new phones."

That's Abbe, and when I wrote to tell her I had André's house for a month she wrote back:

"I'm looking forward to the Second Coming (well, the third). Please save your first Monday evening for dinner at my flat. Monday is my night off."

By June, progess reports had arrived from Ena:

"Muriel Brittain is very excited. Cambridge is pencilled in for 13 August." "The Gommes are delightful. Winchester will be our first trip on 2 August." "The woman in Oxford seems a bid odd."

I'd had a very friendly letter from the woman in Oxford so that last progress report baffled me and I phoned Ena. Leo answered and told me, in his impressive baritone, that Ena was down in the country painting a portrait.

"Has she straightened things out with the woman in Oxford?" I asked.

There was a pause.

"Ena," said Leo, "has everything under control." And he added, "We're both longing to see you."

At the end of June, Doris in the Brighton bookshop wrote to say she would be going "on holiday" on August 6 and hoped we could come one Sunday before then, and I phoned Ena again. Once more, Leo answered. Ena was visiting her mother, who had bronchitis.

"Do you know whether we have the last Sunday in July or the first Sunday in August free — and if not, can we switch one of them?" I asked.

There was a pause.

"Ena," said Leo positively, "would certainly know the answer to that."

On July 19, six days before I was to leave for London, a letter arrived from André:

Dear Helene,

It seems the workmen will be taking over the entire house and you would be uncomfortable there.

But come on the 25th as planned. My mother is in Switzerland for the summer and you will have the use of her flat in St. John's Wood. Penny, my secretary, will meet you at Heathrow and drive you to the flat and turn over the keys to you. . . .

I got out my map of London and literally shouted for joy when I located St. John's Wood. It was at the top of my Visitors' Map — right alongside Regent's Park and a lovely walk down along the park's Outer Circle to Marylebone. I dashed off notes to Ena, Abbe and the fans, and hoped my new address would get to London before I did.

Six days later, with a Nothing book, a date book and all my Best-Laid Plans, I took a night flight to London.

2 a.m. Tues./Wed. 25/26

The first great blessing of a borrowed flat is, if you've
got jet-lag insomnia and you get hungry at two in the
morning, Room Service hasn't closed for the night. I'm at
the kitchen table, I've just had a ham sandwich and a glass
of milk, thanks to Penny, who stocked the refrigerator with
breakfast and lunch supplies for me.

The refrigerator isn't in the kitchen, it's out in the hall.
Standing by itself inside the front door. This flat has several
demented features. They stimulate me.

As we drove here from the airport I asked Penny if she
had Mrs. Deutsch's address in Switzerland so I could write
and thank her for the use of her flat.

"Oh, she doesn't know you're staying there," said Penny.

I thought I'd give myself a holiday from housework over
here, so I said:

"Does she have a cleaning woman I could get to come
in once a week?"

"Mrs. Deutsch likes to do her own cleaning," said Penny.
"She won't let André get her a housekeeper, and of course
it worries him. Not that she's not perfectly healthy. But
she's eighty-eight."

I'll clean it myself.

I'm in a small apartment house just off Wellington Road,
which seems to be the main avenue out here, very wide
and tree-lined. It's a lovely suburb — old houses, old trees,
quiet as the grave at night.

The front door of the flat is at the top of a long narrow
hall that runs the length of the flat, with closets and a

phone table on one side and all the rooms in a row on the other: bedroom, bath, kitchen and, way down at the far end, a large living room.

I got stomped to death in a Customs mob for two hours so it was afternoon when we got here. There was a telegram under the door — WELCOME HOME ENA AND LEO — and a note from Judy Summers about touring Literary Chelsea tomorrow. Penny showed me over the flat and offered me my choice of beds. Mama Deutsch had her big double bed moved into the living room so she could watch television from bed, but I'm sleeping in the single bed in the bedroom. If you've lived in one room all your life, a bedroom is the ultimate luxury.

As soon as Penny left I phoned Ena and she and I shouted at each other excitedly and she said she and Leo would pick me up for dinner at 7:30. Then Diana Athill phoned — she's André's partner — to say there's a Deutsch company lunch for me on Friday.

I don't sleep on planes so after I unpacked I thought I'd take a shower and then try for a nap. But after studying the bathtub I decided a shower wasn't practical. Mama has got the most crowded bathtub you ever saw.

There are thick steel rails with steel handles attached to both rims, for getting in and out; there's a broad wooden bench with steel handles, to sit on while you bathe; and in front of the bench there's a broad rack with soap, sponge, bathbrush and Johnson's Baby Powder. So between the small half-moon of unoccupied tub at the back and the shower nozzle at the front is a wood-and-steel obstacle course I was in no condition to run. I took a bath crouched in the back half-moon.

It wasn't till I stepped out of the bathtub and my toes

curled around it that I noticed Mama's bathroom rug. It's an old Oriental, cut down to fit the bathroom floor. Dripping all over it, I also noticed there were no towels in the bathroom, so I went out into the hall and found the linen closet and opened the door — and my bones melted.

Every shelf is edged with a wide border of white lace, every bundle of sheets, pillow cases, towels and wash cloths is tied in wide pink satin ribbon and finished off with a great pink satin bow.

I can slave an hour wrapping one Christmas present and when I finish, the package looks as if I'd picked it out of a trash can, so I knew I'd be the death of that linen closet. But I'd seen a pile of freshly delivered laundry on the double bed in the living room and there are enough towels and sheets there to last me.

You won't believe this but I just noticed there are Oriental rugs in here, too. In the kitchen. One covers most of the kitchen floor, and there's a little cut-down square piece of another one in front of the stove. You can sit a long time trying to figure out why anyone would want a piece of Oriental carpet in front of the oven. Some other time.

Leo and Ena came up to see the flat and by the time we went down to the lobby it was raining again. Leo had parked the car in the apartment house lot but having the manners of a stately grandee, he insisted on bringing it to the front door for us. And as soon as he left, Ena said:

"I'm going to sit in back with you. Don't say anything about it. I can't sit in the front seat when Leo drives. You don't drive so you woudn't notice it.

"Leo," she went on, "drives straight down the middle of the street. So other cars give him a very wide berth and he's never had an accident. He has the lowest insurance rates in London so of course he thinks he's a very good driver. And I've had accidents, he's certainly not going to listen to me!"

Leo arrived with the car and Ena and I climbed into the back seat. I think the reason why I never noticed his driving is that Leo is so totally imperturbable, behind the wheel as anywhere else, and that kind of temperament inspires confidence in a nondriver. I also never noticed before that Ena is a compulsive back-seat driver. So the conversation on the way to the restaurant went like this:

"We've moved," Leo told me. "My mother died a year ago and left a flat in Park West which we thought we'd sell —"

"Leo, there's a couple crossing the street!"

"— but it's large enough for all Ena's canvases and there's a study for me —"

"Leo, you can't go through. You'll have to turn left."

"— so we're in the process of getting rid of my parents' furniture —"

"Leo! Turn left!"

"— and moving our own things in, to see how we like it —"

"LEFT!"

Leo fell suddenly silent. That's when I noticed our car had stopped. We were in the middle of the street at an intersection and surrounded by heavy traffic. A bus coming toward us had stopped, and a car coming from the right and wanting to cross in front of us had stopped. The bus driver was leaning forward with his arms folded on the wheel, gazing at Leo. The driver trying to cross from the right was leaning out of his car window, staring at Leo.

Suddenly Ena heaved up out of her seat, flung herself

over the back of Leo's seat, reached down and tapped his left wrist.

"THIS is your left hand," she said.

And Leo said tranquilly:

"Thank you, my darling, if you hadn't told me I wouldn't have known."

He surveyed the situation carefully, came to a judicious conclusion and turned left, and we drove the long way to the restaurant. Leo got out of the car, opened the back door and in his courtly fashion helped me out of the car followed by the frayed bundle of nerves beside me.

He isn't going touring with us. He said he has too much work to do. (He was a screenwriter for years, and a play-wright, and somebody in Hollywood is interested in a mod-ernized version of one of his scripts.) Ena says she knew all along he'd back out at the last minute; he hates sight-seeing.

He wanted to know whether the BBC production of "84" had been shown in New York, and while we were talking about it I called the bookshop "Marks and Co." I thought it might sound odd to him, so I said:

"I don't know why, but I've never thought of it as 'Marks and Company.' On their stationery they never spelled out the word 'Company' so I've called it 'Marks and Co' for years, as if 'Co' were a word."

And Leo said in mild surprise:

"You were quite right. The 'Co' didn't stand for com-pany. My uncle, Mark Cohen, was my dad's partner as well as his brother-in-law, so they decided to call the firm 'Marks and Co.' The 'Co' stood for Cohen."

Over coffee, I got out my typewritten list and Ena got out her beautiful chart, with every route and destination in a separate color.

"Did I tell you the woman in Oxford's a bit odd?" Ena asked me.

"Yes, but that's all you said. Odd how?" I asked.

"Well, it seems odd to me," said Ena. "I telephoned her and introduced myself and asked what day she'd like to have us drive up to see Littlemore. And she said — she had a very tense voice — she said she thought it would be much better if Miss Hanff came alone by train."

"Miss Hanff isn't going anywhere alone by train," I said. "She's afraid of getting lost."

"I told her," Ena went on, "that I thought you'd prefer driving through the countryside and she said 'Nonsense' in that tight voice. She said she would meet your train and put you up for the night and I was not to trouble myself further about it."

"I'll call her tomorrow," I said. And Leo said unexpectedly:

"Ena will call her. Ena's in charge of your schedule."

"I really think it's better if I deal with her," said Ena.

We put our lists and chart away and were waiting for the check when Leo said suddenly:

"I wonder what became of the sign that used to hang outside the shop."

I thought of Dan Kelly in Omaha.

"Funny-you-should-ask," I said. "It's hanging on the short wall of my alcove, alongside all the books that came from there."

"That's nice," said Leo peacefully.

This kitchen's going to be my office; it's very sunny in the daytime and the table I'm writing on is solid and roomy. Mama's tea tray was on it: china cream-and-sugar, cup-and-saucer, small pot of honey and a knife and spoon neatly set out on a fresh napkin. I moved the whole tray onto a chair by the window out of harm's way. To anything breakable, I classify as Harm's Way.

Back in my late teens when I was acting with an amateur theatre group, I read a one-act play called *Two Passengers for Chelsea.* It was about Thomas and Jane Carlyle and I loved it. I'd never read Carlyle, so the next day I went to the local library and brought home his *History of the French Revolution.*

All I remember of it is that Carlyle never called Robespierre "Robespierre," he called him "Sea-Green Incorruptible Robespierre" — and I mean if Robespierre was mentioned four times on one page he was "Sea-Green Incorruptible Robespierre" all four times. The whole book was so full of outraged capitals that reading it was like being continuously shouted at. When you finished you were just worn out.

But years later, somebody gave me a book of Jane Carlyle's letters. Till I read them I hadn't known what a huge literary lion Carlyle was, back in the 1840s and '50s. The Carlyle house in Cheyne Row was a literary salon, with Tennyson, Thackeray, Dickens, Emerson, the Brownings, all coming to pay homage to the Sage of Chelsea. Jane presided over the salon with great charm and wit, and her letters took you into that house and made you feel you knew her and Thomas very well. I hadn't known the house still existed and was open to the public — much less that everything in it was exactly as the Carlyles had left it — till Judy Summers took me there this afternoon.

Judy Summers is one of the rare souls who looks exactly

as her name sounds: small, dark-haired, pretty and in her twenties. She quit her job as a tour guide to enroll in a BBC training program. She's learning to edit film, but what she really wants to be is a novelist.

"If I'm trained for a job that pays well, like film editing," she said, "I'll be able to work half the year and save enough to live on the other half while I write."

She can probably manage it. Her parents own a house in St. John's Wood, and Judy has a floor of it converted into a flat, rent-free.

The trouble with Literary Chelsea is that except for the Carlyle house, none of the literary houses you want to see are open to the public. We stopped outside one, for instance, and Judy pointed up to the third floor.

"D'you see those two windows on the left?" she asked me. "They were the windows to Henry James's study."

We stopped in front of another house and Judy jabbed an accusing finger at the living-room curtains behind which we could see someone moving.

"You'll notice there are people living there," she said. "They can do anything they like with that house! It's not a museum, it's not National Trust. And the powers-that-be hope you won't notice the plaque. The name on it isn't pure enough for the house to be preserved!"

The house belonged to Oscar Wilde.

Then we went to Cheyne Row and walked into a sitting room that's exactly as the artist painted it in the painting reproduced in my book of Jane's letters. There was the busy wallpaper and busy slipcovers you know Jane chose because they wouldn't show the dirt and wouldn't wear out with too much cleaning (she was monstrous thrifty), and the horde of knickknacks on the mantel. And the small sofa where Nero, the family dog, sat for the only portrait in the painting Jane approved of.

What that painter put her through was a refined form of torture. Jane spent most of her time in the sitting room; she had to do all her letter-writing, sewing and meal-planning there because it was the only room where her movements didn't disturb the Genius working upstairs in his study. Well, the painter wanted to paint the living room and part of the dining room seen through the doorway — in microscopic detail — and he came two days a week for three months and then every day for six more weeks. And painted at Jane's elbow.

The chair is still there, near the door as it is in the painting, as it was on the day Jane jumped up from it when Leigh Hunt came.

The Hunts lived around the corner and Leigh used to drop in regularly. But he was sick one winter and was absent for so long that when he finally recovered and appeared in the Carlyles' doorway, Jane jumped up and kissed him. And a day or two later, one of the Hunt servants delivered a note. From Mr. Hunt to Mrs. Carlyle. The note read:

> *Jenny kissed me when we met,*
> *Jumping from the chair she sat in;*
> *Time, you thief, who love to get*
> *Sweets into your list, put that in:*
>
> *Say I'm weary, say I'm sad,*
> *Say that health and wealth have missed me,*
> *Say I'm growing old, but add*
> *Jenny kissed me.*

I think he was the only one who called her Jenny. Her friends and family, including Thomas, called her Jeannie.

The house is full of lovely paneled walls and spacious rooms, but the only other room I identified with was Thomas's study at the top of the house, because of what Jane went through to build it.

She spent half her time trying to keep the house quiet so Thomas could work in peace. She kept herself and the servants out of earshot, she bribed and threatened the neighbors into selling their noisy poultry and playing their piano only at specified hours — and still the house wasn't quiet enough. So one season when Thomas went away on a three-month lecture tour, Jane decided to surprise him by building a new study for him at the top of the house. She hired workmen to build new walls, new windows, new fireplace, and when the workmen were too slow, she pitched in and helped them build it. Then she installed Thomas's desk and bookshelves and made curtains and cushions and slipcovers — and completed the study triumphantly the day before Thomas came home.

He couldn't work in it. It wasn't quiet enough.

So Thomas magnanimously went away for another month, to give Jane a chance to rip out the new walls and the new fireplace and help the workmen install soundproofing. After that, it was finally quiet enough for Thomas to finish his definitive five-volume life of Frederick the Great.

Jane was a pretty fair writer herself. I can't quote any of the letters from memory, but I've got a passage of her journal by heart. Carlyle was infatuated with a Lady Ashburton and the infatuation lasted twenty years, at least, until the lady's death. Lord and Lady Ashburton lived at Bath House.

"That eternal Bath House," Jane wrote in her journal.

"I wonder how many thousand miles Mr. C. has walked between there and here. Oh, when I first noticed that heavy yellow house, without knowing or caring who it belonged to, how far I was from dreaming that through years and years, I should carry every stone's weight of it on my heart."

We're doing the Abbey on Saturday. Ena wants to tour the Tower with us and she's painting somebody on Saturday.

Harrow tomorrow.

Thursday evening, July 27

Peter Astaire called for me at eleven a.m. as planned. He came alone. He's beautiful in the way all English public school boys seem to be at fifteen: dark hair carefully cut to frame a chiseled face, beautiful manners — and absolute self-possession.

"My mother will meet us at the tube station in half an hour," he said. He told me his father and two older brothers went to Harrow, which made me nervous. I had a feeling my best pantsuit wasn't suitable for lunching with the wife of one Harrovian and the mother of three more, but I couldn't help it. I'm stuck with heavy clodhopper shoes and I don't wear skirts or dresses, they look hideous with oxfords.

"We lived in St. John's Wood when I was small," he said. "I thought I'd take you on a tour of the neighborhood and show you where to find everything that's not in the High Street. The High Street's just round the corner, you'll find that easily. All the shops there are good."

And we set off on a tour of what wasn't on the High Street. He took me to the post office and showed me how to use the stamp machine. He pointed out the best dry-cleaner's, the fastest dry-cleaner's, the launderette, the off-license (liquor store) — "There's one in the High Street but this one's a bit closer if it's raining or near closing time" — and the "local," the pub he said was "the best in St. John's Wood." Then we walked to the tube station.

There was no middle-aged woman waiting for us. What there was, sitting behind the wheel of an Alfa Romeo, was a slim, pretty redhead in her thirties, in an unpressed linen dress the color of the freckles on her nose.

"This is my mother," said Peter. And the redhead said, "I'm Lesley," and stuck out a hand shyly.

"You must have been a child bride!" I said as I climbed in the back seat. Lesley said:

"Almost. I was married at eighteen and had my oldest son at nineteen."

We had lunch at what both of them told me was "the best fish-and-chips pub in London" and then drove to Harrow-on-the-Hill in bright sunshine. It was a short drive through green suburban country. Then the car climbed a long uphill road. At the top of it, there was Harrow-on-the-Hill, a picture postcard. You come first to the King's Head Hotel, built in 1535, and a few yards from it, a gibbet with Henry VIII's portrait (the king's head) hanging from it, which seemed a kind of ambiguous compliment to the school's founder — or patron, I'm not sure which.

Just beyond the hotel on a rise above a great lawn is Harrow School. It's a red brick mansion, with two imposing white stone staircases, one on either side, curving up to the white arched door, and a white turret clock set in the red brick above the door. While Peter mounted the steps and rang for the caretaker, Lesley and I waited on the lawn below. I told her how impressed I was with his aplomb.

"He wouldn't let me come to your flat with him," she told me. "He said: 'I think Helene and I ought to have a little time to ourselves first, Mother. We'll meet you at half-past eleven.'" So she'd waited meekly at the tube station.

The caretaker came to the door and we saw him and Peter in conversation. The conversation lengthened. Then the caretaker went back into the school building, closing the door behind him, and Peter came slowly back to us.

"The caretaker says he's not permitted to allow visitors to go through the building in summer when the school's closed," he said. "Not even with a Harrow student to escort them." And then he said: "If you don't mind sitting on the grass, I can tell Helene all about the school and answer any of her questions."

My heart went out to him. He'd counted on showing me Harrow. But without batting an eye he proceeded to give me a history of the school — "Lord Byron, Winston Churchill and King Hussein all went to Harrow" — and then told me about the dormitories, called Houses.

"You're put down for a certain House by your parents as soon as you're born. My father and brothers were all at Headmaster House, so of course that's where I am."

He said the salaries paid to teachers — called "masters" — are "appalling."

"Harrow attracts some of the best masters because it pays the best," he said. "But even at Eton and Harrow, the masters must have small private incomes to manage decently. At Oxford and Cambridge the pay is so poor most of the professors are impoverished."

He said most of the kids smoke pot — "and we all know which masters drink."

He confirmed something I'd guessed from what little I'd read about English schools and universities and it baffles me. There's no such thing as a graduation ceremony — not at Eton or Harrow or Oxford or Cambridge.

"You stay until you finish the course and then you leave."

What baffles me is where, in the former English colonies I live in, the great American Graduation Day came from. We make so much of high school graduations and college commencements we must have got them from somewhere.

After the lecture, Peter took us for a walk along the High Street — a hilly road lined with shops in Tudor houses. He pointed out "the tuck shop" (candy store) and the restaurant — blandly named "The Old Etonian." Then we went into the official school clothing store so Lesley could order a few things Peter needed. While we stood at the counter, she and Peter conferred, and then Peter announced they were buying me a Harrow School shirt. It's white with a thin blue stripe — in the kind of fine sheer wool I haven't seen since nylon/orlon/dacron and all their miserable ilk took over the world.

We left the High Street for a wider avenue lined with the Houses. They might be turn-of-the-century New York mansions or small-town city halls, red or grey stone buildings with white-columned doorways and none of the institutional look of American dormitories.

We drove back to Kensington. Peter wanted to show me his books about New York and Lesley wanted me to have tea in their garden. I'd heard about Cassius, the family terrier, and as Lesley put her key in the lock an outraged high-pitched barking started on the other side of the door. I figured it was hearing my strange voice that set him off so I stooped down and lifted the mail slot. All I could see through the opening was a white tail waving, but I called:

"Hi, Cassius!" From which Cassius concluded we must have met somewhere and become friends, and when we walked in he greeted me with enthusiasm.

(It occurs to me I do exactly the same thing. Some out-of-town fan will phone and say:

"Miss Hanff? It's Mary Jones from Seattle."
And I don't know her but she obviously knows me so I say:

"How *are* you?" With enthusiasm.)

Rain routed us out of the garden and when I left I wished them better luck with the weather in Cornwall; they're off on a two-week vacation tomorrow.

Friday, 28th

I just went marketing in St. John's Wood High Street. You're walking along an ordinary twentieth-century street, you turn right, into the High Street, and you're back in Jane Austen's day. It's a two-block stretch of small, sedate shops with decorous shop windows — no big signs, no gaudy displays — all of it looking so gentle and well-bred you want to take slow, ladylike steps. I walked up one side of the street and back down the other, past bakeries, meat markets, vegetable markets, gift shops, florist shops, china store, dress shop, shoe store, stationery store, an optometrist's, and two small supermarkets.

I went into one of the supermarkets and I didn't hit trouble till I'd filled my cart and pushed it to the checkout counter. I put all my purchases on the counter and the clerk added up the total and I paid him. I waited for him to pack everything in bags but he just stood there, and the two of us stared at each other, both waiting. Finally he said:

"Where's your bag?"

In London you take your own plastic bag to the supermarket with you. I explained I hadn't known this, and the clerk produced a couple of bags from a hidden supply and packed everything, but he made it clear I'd ruined his morning.

When I got back here and put my coffee and tea and crackers in the kitchen supply closet, I found Mama's bag supply. On the inside of the closet door there's a round nylon net bag stuffed to globe size with hundreds of plastic bags, each one folded neatly very small. She must have been saving them for twenty years.

Then I watered the 47 plants — every windowsill is crammed with them — and went into the bedroom to dress for the Deutsch company lunch. The bedroom has my favorite batty feature.

The room is dominated by a massive free-standing mahogany wardrobe Mama must have brought with her from Hungary fifty years ago. It's finished off at the top with an intricately carved railing. Well, behind the railing, lined up in a neat row are five empty egg cartons. Three paper, two plastic. If you're sitting on the bed putting on your pantyhose you can waste a lot of time staring at those egg cartons trying to figure out what they're doing there.

If you need to buy pantyhose over here, you ask for "tights."

Later

André's offices are in a five-story brownstone on Great Russell Street and the top floor is a large empty room reserved for literary sherry parties and company lunches. Diana, André's partner, presided at the lunch and everybody was there: Bill the sales manager, Piers the negotiator, Pam the Juvenile editor, and my personal Prince Philip, Deutsch's business manager and my private banker when I'm here. "Oh, don't bother the bank, dear," he says, and doles out cash to me every week and deducts it from my next royalty check.

This company lunch would not be possible in New York because, though your editor is in a New York skyscraper, if your publisher is Lippincott, the sales manager and business manager are in Philadelphia. If it's Doubleday, they're out on Long Island. If it's Little, Brown, they're in Boston.

Futura, the paperback house that publishes my books over here, is also having a company lunch for me. Next Friday.

Saturday, July 29

Do not put off paying for that crypt or grave you ordered for yourself. Consider what happened to Ben Jonson.

Ben knew he'd be entitled to burial in Westminster Abbey and he reserved a grave there for himself and he never paid for it. Well, when he died he had a fine funeral and then the mourners went home and left Ben to be buried in his crypt under the Abbey floor. But the grave-diggers knew he hadn't paid for it, and they weren't going to waste valuable grave space on a deadbeat. So they opened the grave and slid Ben in, upright, and propped him in a corner, to keep the grave available for a paying customer.

This was in 1637 but nobody knew about it till 1793.

"In 1793," reported Judy, "the grave was opened to put

a man named John Hunter in it — and the grave-diggers saw Ben Jonson's red hair sticking up out of the corner."

"What did they do with him?" I asked.

"Nothing," said Judy. "They just left him standing there."

You think of the old bromides about Eternal Rest — "How sleep the brave who sink to rest"; "We shall rest, and, faith, we shall need it — lie down for an aeon or two . . ." They all go right out the window when you realize Ben Jonson is spending Eternity standing up.

He had no luck whatever in Westminster Abbey; even the plaque in his memory has to be hidden away in a side wall where the Abbey hopes nobody will see it because the eulogy on it begins:

"O rare Ben Johnson"

and that ain't how he spelled it.

Still, he was a lot luckier than Oliver Cromwell. Judy took me into the Henry VII Chapel and pointed to a sign:

THE BURIAL PLACE OF OLIVER CROMWELL

"It's his burial place," she said, "but it's not his grave."

The Lord Protector was buried there in 1658 with great pomp. But two years later came the restoration of the monarchy. And Charles II, whose father had been beheaded by Cromwell, had the body dug up and sentenced to be half-hanged, drawn and quartered for high treason. So Cromwell's decomposing corpse was publicly disemboweled and carved up. Thousands of Londoners came to the festivities.

I saw the tomb in which Elizabeth and her half-sister Queen Mary are buried together, in spite of the fact that Elizabeth was sent to the Tower on Bloody Mary's orders. She wanted to write to Mary and ask to be put to death by a French executioner's sword instead of an English axe, because a sword sliced a head off in one clean blow and an axe didn't. How Elizabeth knew this is that when she was three years old, her mother, Ann Boleyn, had died by a French sword and somehow Elizabeth learned it had been a quick, clean death. When she was eight, the one stepmother she loved — Catherine Howard — had her head clumsily hacked off by repeated blows of the axe.

I was very moved to find memorials to two American writers there:

HENRY JAMES, O.M.
Novelist
New York, 1843
London, 1916

THOMAS STEARNS ELIOT, O.M.
Born 26 Sept., 1888
Died 4 Jan., 1965

On the way to the Abbey, we stopped at the Hotel Cadogan — Judy having discovered I love Oscar Wilde's plays and *The Ballad of Reading Gaol.* The hotel is still elegant and expensive but Judy said that back in the 1890s it was the most exclusive hotel in London.

"This is where the police came to arrest him," she said. "One of the arresting officers stepped up to him and said in a low voice:

" 'Please come quietly, Mr. Wilde, this *is* the Cadogan.' "

We're doing the Tower next Friday if Ena can make it. Abbe just phoned to confirm dinner Monday night.

"222 Sandringham Flats, Charing Cross Road," she said. "Are you sure you can find it?"

I told her not to insult me.

Brighton tomorrow.

It was raining this morning when Ena came and we called Doris in Brighton. She said it was raining there, too, and she and Ena agreed that Brighton was a town to see on foot so we waited to see what the weather would do.

Ena loves Mama's kitchen mantel. It has a long row of Mama's treasures — painted china plates, pewter cream-and-sugar, souvenirs André brought her from faraway places — with kitchen necessities tucked unobtrusively between them, and even those — spice jars, soap dish, cleaning cloths — are all carefully chosen and arranged. One item baffled me. The centerpiece is a polished pewter teapot, and on one side of it, hanging down on a short string, is a large round medal with "Mary" (Mama's name) on it. But on the other side there's a round Christmas tree ball, also on a string.

"Why would she hang a Christmas tree ornament up there?" I asked Ena.

"For balance," she said. "Mama likes symmetry. She probably couldn't find anything else the same size and shape as the medal."

Ena made a detailed drawing of the mantel for me and entertained me with Leo stories while she worked.

"We had a cottage in Dorking last summer, it was on the water, and one day Leo decided to take the dinghy out and read while he floated.

"He piled his books in the dinghy carefully — you know how measured his movements are; none of this was hurried — he piled the books very neatly, edge to edge, and then he stepped majestically into the dinghy. But he didn't step into the middle of it the way anyone else would. He stepped onto one end of it. And the other end rose very slowly into the air — and Leo, in absolute slow motion, went perfectly head-over-ass into the water. It was lovely to watch!" And she went off into peals of laughter at the memory.

"Did he get mad when you laughed?" I asked.

"Oh, no, not Leo!" said Ena. "He just picked himself up, dignified as ever. Then he shook the water out of each book, piled them carefully back into the dinghy and then stepped into the middle of it, dripping wet but majestic as ever, and sailed off."

She said he also decided to take up horseback riding down there.

"On the day of his first lesson he got on the horse with a cigar in his mouth. It was all right: the horse refused to move. Either he didn't like the cigar smoke or he didn't like Leo." And she was off on another fit of laughter. "The instructor was quite upset and embarrassed but Leo wasn't perturbed in the least. He just handed me his cigar and politely asked for another horse."

At one o'clock it was still raining in both cities and we postponed Brighton till next Sunday. Doris insists she's not leaving on vacation till Monday.

Monday, July 31
lunchtime

I rose up early this morning to clean the flat and started by putting the kitchen and bathroom Oriental rugs out in the hall so I could scrub the floors. Then I went looking for the bucket. I looked in every kitchen and hall closet. No bucket anywhere. What I found instead was a toy-sized Bissell rug-shampooer so light a child could push it — and bottles and bottles of carpet shampoo. Even so, it wasn't till I was wiping the steel handrails on the bathtub that the obvious hit me.

Mama must be arthritic. She can't bend and straighten easily or she wouldn't need the hand rails. So of course she can't get down on her knees to scrub floors. But she was by God gonna do her floors herself — even if it meant cutting down her Oriental rugs to fit them, including an extra patch of rug in front of the stove.

Ena phoned; she switched dates so she can do the Tower with us next Friday. I called Futura to ask if I could bring her to the company lunch and Futura said: "Any relation of Marks & Co. is welcome at Futura." I figure if she's along, we'll get out of there in time to meet Judy at two.

It's raining and Ena insists on driving me in to Charing Cross Road tonight for dinner with Abbe. She said she's meeting Leo in town anyway.

9 p.m.

I've given up sitting by the phone waiting for Abbe to call and ask what happened. I'm in the living room. I thought if I watched TV it might calm me down but it didn't. I turned it off and I'm just sitting, cursing the London phone company for not giving Abbe a phone.

Charing Cross Road is two streets long. Ena drove slowly down it, peering out the window on her side while I peered out the window on mine, looking for Sandringham Flats. There was nothing that looked like an apartment house.

In spite of the rush-hour traffic Ena circled around a couple of one-way streets and then drove back down Charing Cross Road slowly, twice, and neither of us found any sign of Sandringham Flats. Finally I told her to drop me at the upper end of the road and I'd find the place on foot.

Ena drove off and I walked slowly down one side of the road and then slowly back up the other side, but all I passed were small shops, none of which carried the numbers 222 or the name Sandringham Flats. And I blame Suburbia for what happened next.

The bookshops had closed for the day, but most stores were open — record shops, souvenir shops, a photo store, a couple of fast-food places. I went into the first one and asked the clerk if he could tell me where Sandringham Flats was. He'd never heard of it.

"D'you have the street name?" he asked me.

"It's on Charing Cross Road," I said.

This shook him. He gawked a minute and then shouted to somebody in the back:

"Bill! Lady's lookin' for Sandringham Flats!"

Bill never heard of it.

I went into every single open store on both sides of Charing Cross Road — and not one clerk or manager could point out an apartment house on the street they both worked on five days a week. I thought it was only in New York that suburbanites took a commuter train every morning into the city, worked all day in stores or offices and took the commuter train home in the evening without ever seeing or learning anything of the street they worked on.

At seven, I was still wandering up and down Charing Cross Road. At seven-fifteen, I went into one of the snack bars and ate a sandwich standing at the window in case Abbe came by looking for me.

At eight, I took a cab back up here and sat by the phone — in tears — hoping she'd call from a phone booth.

Of all the roads in London I had to get lost on that one.

Abbe phoned. She said she "hung around the gate" for an hour and then went up and ate her company dinner by herself.

"What gate?" I said.

"There's an entrance gate with the name cut into it, but it's iron and so old and dark nobody can see it," she said. "You're not the first one who couldn't find us. I keep bringing it up at tenants' meetings and demanding we put up a large modern sign. But there's always some elderly wardrobe mistress who says: 'People who can't find us don't deserve to.' That's why I asked if you were sure you could find it. If you hadn't been so superior about it I'd have given you directions."

I'm taking her to theatre and a late dinner next Monday to make up for it. She'll meet me in front of 84, Charing Cross Road:

"You can find *that?*"

Now I know why it's rained every day since I landed. It must have rained on July 15, which is St. Swithun's day. I just read the booklet the Gommes bought me at Winchester Cathedral. St. Swithun is the cathedral's patron saint and what it says in the booklet is:

St. Swithun's Day, if thou dost rain,
For forty days it will remain;
St. Swithun's Day, if thou be fair
For forty days 'twill rain nae mair.

— sort of a summer Groundhog's Day.

We met the Gommes at an inn for lunch. Jim is a retired headmaster, and Jean bowled me over by telling me she grew up in one of the Nash Crescent houses in Regent's Park back in the days of large families and nannies and live-in servants.

We went to the cathedral after lunch and the Gommes took me straight to Izaak Walton's little alcove. The main feature is a three-panel stained-glass memorial. A neat sign underneath it says:

"The Gift of the Fishermen of the World."

You stare at the sign and imagine all the anonymous fishermen from Maine to Dover to Marseilles to the coasts of Scotland and Australia and California and Newfoundland chipping in their pounds and francs and dollars to create a memorial to the world's most famous Angler.

The central panel was of portraits of the "fishers of men" whose short biographies Walton wrote in the *Lives*. But the pane I stared at longest was the one with a portrait of Izaak himself. He's sitting reading with his fishing-rod, net and creel beside him. And the serenity of the face reminded me of his line about the milkmaid:

"She does not worry about things which will not be."

Considering that he lived from King James I's day, through the beheading of Charles I, then helped an Anglican churchman escape from Lord Protector Cromwell and lived on into the Restoration, he must have spent most of his life not worrying about things which might have happened to him but didn't.

Ena and the Gommes had tactfully left me alone in there and I started down a long side aisle looking for them, with one eye on the stone graves I was walking on. That's how I came on Jane Austen's grave. To look down at a spot in a stone floor and know that Jane lies buried beneath it can shake you. Then I read the long inscription her brothers and sister wrote for the tombstone — and got apoplectic.

> The benevolence of her heart, the sweetness of her temper and the extraordinary endowments of her mind obtained the regard of all who knew her, and the warmest love of her intimate connections.

— and another paragraph about the family's grief and their confidence that her soul would be "acceptable in the sight of her Redeemer."

The whole epitaph was the sort of effusion any family might write about any sister. No indication whatever that this particular sister wrote books — that "obtained the regard of" a helluva lot of people who *didn't* know her.

Then we drove to Jane's house at Chawton, and the tablet on the brick wall there made up for the family's oversight.

> JANE AUSTEN
> Lived here from 1809 to 1817 and hence all her works were sent into the world. Her admirers in this country and in America have united to erect this tablet.

And you open the door and walk into the house whence all her books were sent into the world.

The door of the sitting room has been carefully trained to creak for tourists who know that it creaked in Jane's day and she wouldn't let anyone oil it because the warning creak told her company had come and gave her a chance to hide her current manuscript before the visitors entered the room.

We climbed the stairs to Jane's bedroom. There's a dress of the period lying across the bed and several more on mannequins. One white muslin dress with puffed sleeves and an embroidered bouffant skirt reminded me of Lydia Bennet's moronic note telling her friends she was eloping with Wickham and asking them to have a servant "mend a great slit in my worked muslin gown." And we saw the white housecaps Jane wore, including the one from which she looks out at you in the portrait in the front of most editions of her books.

On one of the upstairs walls, in a small frame, there's a letter written by Jane to tell her brother Edward that their father was dead, breaking the news so gently the letter carries its own balm.

Our dear father has closed his virtuous and happy life in a manner almost as free of suffering as his children could have wished. . . .

When we came downstairs we went out to the back yard to see the bake-house, the copper-lined pit for washing clothes and the huge iron wash basin near the pump. I wish I'd thought to ask the caretaker about a kitchen item Jane mentioned. In one of her books, she described a kitchen as being fitted with all the latest modern conveniences including "a hot-closet." I'd love to know what a "hot-closet" was.

The Gommes took us home to their airy country house in Farnham for tea. The living room has a stone fireplace with armchairs and a sofa in a semicircle in front of it. But the weather was clear and we had tea in the garden — scones and jam and strawberries and double-cream — and they'd gone out and bought gin and vermouth for me in case I wanted to top off tea with a martini.

A two-minute walk from the house is a small cottage, "where," said Jean Gomme tranquilly, "one of us will live when the other one dies."

Ena's still having trouble with the woman in Oxford.

"I talked to her again last night," she said. "I told her we'd like to come down on Tuesday or Wednesday of next week and asked which of the two days was more convenient for her. And she said: 'Just tell Miss Hanff to take the ten o'clock train on whichever day suits her. She can let me know by postcard.'"

So I just wrote her a friendly letter saying it seemed silly to come by train when Ena had offered to drive me through the countryside, and we'd like to come on Tuesday and would arrive about noon and I was very excited about seeing Littlemore.

Friday, August 4

Once upon a time, two children eight years old — a girl named Elizabeth, a boy named Robert, called Rob — were introduced to each other and told that they had been born on the same day and at the same hour and that Fate would therefore give them parallel destinies. They grew up in the same small circle of noble families, so, when the twenty-year-old Elizabeth was taken as a prisoner to the Tower, she knew that Rob was already a prisoner there.

That's the beginning of the romance of Queen Elizabeth I and Rob Dudley, the only man she was to love till the day she died.

(Don't annoy me with Essex. Rob Dudley died at fifty-eight, and Elizabeth turned for solace to his asinine stepson, Lord Essex. But she didn't hesitate to have Essex put to death when he tried to overthrow her. And at her own death, when the locked box she always kept on her bedside table was finally opened, all it contained was a letter from Rob with the notation in Elizabeth's hand: "The last letter he ever wrote.")

I'd told Judy what I wanted to see most in the Tower and she took Ena and me to the Beauchamp Tower first. At the bottom of the entrance stairs she showed us the name, "Robart [*sic*] Dudley," which Rob cut into the stone before climbing to his prison quarter. The winding stone staircase is fearsome. You climb steep steps between huge stone walls that get grimmer and darker at every landing.

We came to Rob's landing and Judy led the way into "the Dudley apartments" — a bland name for a sixteenth-century prison cell with stone walls several feet thick. You try to imagine what it was like when darkness closed in and candles threw long shadows on the grey stone walls.

There's a narrow outdoor walkway outside the Dudley apartments connecting the Beauchamp Tower to the Bell Tower, where Elizabeth was held. Every day, with two guards in front of her and two behind, Elizabeth was allowed to walk the length of the passage for exercise. When she reached the far end, she was outside Rob's room. She knew he was listening behind the stone wall and could hear her footsteps, and her voice if she spoke to a guard, and would be cheered by her presence as she was by his. On that walkway I paid homage to the two of them for all I owe them.

It's my belief that if Elizabeth hadn't encouraged Sir Humphrey Gilbert and Sir Walter Raleigh to explore the New World, I'd have been born speaking Spanish instead of speaking (unrecognizably, to be sure) the tongue that Shakespeare spoke. Well, that's of importance to nobody but me. What's important to half the world is that thanks to Elizabeth, Shakespeare was free to speak the tongue that Shakespeare spoke, as an actor/playwright on a public stage. She was the first English monarch who loved the theatre and encouraged it instead of ordering sheriffs to hound the players out of town. Now Rob Dudley wasn't exactly anybody's parfit gentil knight. He was devious, calculating and untrustworthy, whether he ordered his wife's death or not. (She either fell down a long flight of stairs, or was pushed down them by a servant at Rob's suggestion.) All that matters to me about Rob Dudley is that he was the Earl of Leicester, patron of Shakespeare's company.

From Rob's landing we went to the White Tower, where the main torture room and the dungeons were, but there's nothing to see there anymore. The dungeons are closed to the public now, and the torture devices have been replaced on the torture room walls by ancient weapons and suits of armor. Which was fine with me. I'm not just crazy about torture chambers, and I've read more than I wanted to know about men and women having their legs and arms stretched on the rack till every joint was pulled out of its socket and every bone broken.

We went out of doors to Tower Green, a lovely small park where royal beheadings took place, including those of three young queens: Anne Boleyn, Catherine Howard and Lady Jane Grey.

Weaker Sex note: Lady Jane Grey, aged sixteen, went to her execution with what witnesses called superhuman grace and courage. She comforted the clergyman who was there to comfort her and asked the swordsman for instruction so she could place her head on the block correctly.

Her nineteen-year-old husband (Rob Dudley's brother) cried all the way to the scaffold.

Her father was another winner. He'd forced Jane to accept the crown she didn't want and wasn't entitled to — and as soon as she was arrested, he denounced her, to save his own skin.

Royal executions on Tower Green were private. Ordinary traitors were executed on Tower Hill, outside the Tower precincts, and the block was on a scaffold built good and high so ten thousand Londoners could see the show. They jammed the hill and perched in trees to get a good look at the axe or sword as it fell, and see the head roll off and the blood gush out. Then they stampeded up to the scaffold with pieces of rag to dip in the blood. You wouldn't believe how many diseases were cured by the blood of executed traitors.

I finally found out what the "Order of the Bath" means. Meant. Judy took us to a 900-year-old church on the second floor of the White Tower called the Chapel of St. John.

"This is where the Knights of the Bath prayed before their investiture," she said. "After the service, they were ushered into an adjoining room where they stripped and bathed in wooden tubs. As they sat in their tubs the King entered, tapped the bare shoulder of each man with a sword and declared him a Knight of the Bath."

Then Queen Mary ascended the throne, followed by

Elizabeth, and the ritual had to be abandoned since no female monarch could be asked to enter a room full of naked men sitting in bathtubs.

No other tourist attraction I've ever heard of has the grotesque contrasts of the Tower. The sumptuous royal apartments where monarchs once stayed from the day they inherited the throne to the day of their Coronation were above torture rooms and dungeons and had a fine view of the bloodletting on Tower Green. I was glad we didn't line up to see the Crown Jewels; it would have been like seeing the Taj Mahal and Auschwitz on the same day.

We rescued my beautiful flowers from the Tower cloakroom, lugged them to Brown's Hotel, and checked them at the cloakroom there while we had tea. They were half dead when I got them home but they're in water and recovering. They were presented to me at the Futura company lunch.

Futura has the youngest executives I've ever met. They're all in their twenties, sleek, groomed, buttoned-down young men of the kind called Upwardly Mobile at home.

I sat next to the editor-in-chief and he told me he's sorry they published *84* and *The Duchess* in one paperback volume.

"We thought *84, Charing Cross Road* was too short to publish by itself at the usual paperback price," he said. "Now we know we could easily have sold the two books in separate volumes and of course we'd have done much better financially."

So I told him my favorite Writer's Economics lesson:

"Every reader who buys your paperback with the two books in it writes me a fan letter and I write a thank-you note to each of them," I said. "My thank-you note costs twenty-two cents; my royalty on the book is eleven cents;

so every time somebody buys the book I lose eleven cents."

And he said:

"You're lucky to be getting eleven cents. If the paperback contained one book instead of two, you'd get only seven cents."

On my back he's Upwardly Mobile.

Brighton was rained out again yesterday. Doris was so disappointed. I think she postponed her holiday for a weekend just to show it to me. Ena says she's going to drive me down on the first sunny day we have free. She didn't tell me before that she knows the city and loves it.

A letter in the mail from the woman in Oxford. She's been called out of town by the illness of a cousin and she can't say how long she'll be gone. She's so sorry to miss meeting me.

Well, she's not the first puzzle I've run into in my life. I tell myself with fans as with the weather, you win a few, you lose a few.

Abbe met me outside the empty storefront at 84 — which the owners won't let to anybody because they want to tear it down. It's a good thing she knew me because I'd have walked right past her. She's acquired a slim figure, lustrous long hair, contact lenses and complete self-possession. And the damnedest English accent you ever heard. Most of the time she speaks with the impeccable accent she hears onstage. Then she'll come on something that surprises her and say:

"Oh, Gawd!"

in the half-cockney she must hear backstage.

You'll never stumble on Sandringham Flats, you have to know where to look for it. It's not on Charing Cross Road, it's set back behind it. It's a long row of flats in a heavy brown building with high iron gates.

We climbed outdoor stone steps, four flights of them, to get to 222. On each of the three landings we passed was a broad stone walkway with all the flats on the landing opening onto it, giving all the tenants a kind of community balcony. On the fourth floor, Abbe led the way across the walkway into her flat.

The real estate developers keep declaring Sandringham Flats unfit for human habitation, and Abbe knows she won't have hers for very long: there's a rumor that the telephone company was right and the flats on Abbe's side of the street are to be torn down soon. It's a pity. She has a bright, clean apartment — living room, bedroom, kitchen and "loo." She painted all the rooms herself, she bought carpeting and cut it and tacked it down very professionally and she's created a warm and attractive home. With no bathtub and no shower stall.

"I don't know why Americans make such a fuss about bathtubs," she said testily. "You get just as clean taking sponge baths."

"Americans" forsooth.

Wednesday, August 9

I just read the booklets I brought home from Brighton last night, all about Prinny and Mrs. Fitzherbert, and Prinny is now, after Elizabeth I, my favorite English monarch.

"Prinny" was the nickname of the Prince Regent who became George IV. When he was young he fell in love with a pretty Catholic widow, Mrs. Fitzherbert, and since the English constitution forbade the future king's marriage to a Roman Catholic, young George married Mrs. Fitzherbert secretly. When he became Regent, he regretfully stopped living with her, and by the time he was crowned George IV he'd made a proper royal marriage. Without benefit of a divorce. The marriage was unhappy and the King — still called Prinny by his friends — consoled himself with a string of mistresses. But when he died, it was Mrs. Fitzherbert's portrait they found in a locket around his neck.

What I love most about this story is the vision of Mrs. Fitzherbert going placidly through life knowing the Queen of England was married to a bigamist. All of which has nothing whatever to do with why Prinny's my second favorite monarch.

He had a consuming passion for architecture. As Prince Regent he commissioned John Nash to turn an old house at Windsor into Windsor Castle, and then directed him to cut a great royal swath through the green fields of London. On Prinny's orders, Nash built a long avenue — calling it Regent Street, of course — with Carlton House Terrace at its lower end and at the top end Regent's Park, with facing crescents of white houses flanking the entrance, and a series of terraces of tall white houses along the Outer Circles of the park. All this and Brighton Pavilion, too. But Doris was right. You don't go to Brighton just to see the Pavilion.

It was a beautiful day and Ena and I drove down before the weather could change its mind. Outside Brighton we came to a detour and went through a lush green suburb called Hove, along a boulevard lined with red brick Victorian houses with white-trimmed bay windows and white porches. Then we turned a corner and suddenly there was the sea, very calm and blue, and Ena said:

"This is Brighton."

When I was a child, my family took a house in Atlantic City every summer. I'd never liked it much — but by the time Ena parked the car inland, I was suddenly wild to get back to the seashore and we went there first.

It looked both strange and familiar. "The boardwalk" above the surf in Atlantic City is literally made of wooden boards on wooden stilts. In Brighton, the promenade deck is concrete and the railing is wrought-iron. Then I looked down at the "beach," and got a jolt. It's not made of sand, it's made of pebbles — thousands of them as far as the eye reaches along the shore. And sunbathers stretched out on the burning hot pebbles as peacefully as Indian holy men on beds of nails.

We strolled along the promenade, past a row of Victorian beachfront hotels smaller than the Atlantic City palaces of my childhood but just as gaudy. One of them had bright red awnings at every single window. I couldn't remember when I'd last seen an awning.

When we left the beachfront, Ena took me through hilly little shopping streets, more Cape Cod than Atlantic City, with small curio shops, gift shops, snack bars all pasted up against each other in winding rows. Then we came to a big corner store that sold nothing but Brighton Rock.

"I always thought Brighton Rock was a boulder, like Plymouth Rock," I told Ena.

"It may well have been, originally," said Ena.

What it is now is hard candy. It comes in great, round, flat lollypops, but mostly you buy it in long striped rolls like miniature barber poles. Red-and-white, red-and-green, red-yellow-and-green, six inches long or two feet long, it's as unique to Brighton as salt-water taffy is to Atlantic City.

What moved me unexpectedly was that the Brighton Rock candy palace looked like the salt-water taffy stores. It was large, open on all sides and swarming with teenagers in bathing suits and bare feet. Some of them had "punk" orange or purple hair, some of the boys had shaved "skin-heads" — but they were essentially the same teenagers I'd looked up to when I was eight years old, the same thin tanned bodies, the same exuberant self-absorbed faces as they jostled their decorous elders. The proper middle-aged patrons were the same, the holiday atmosphere was the same — and from the opposite shore my eight-year-old self never dreamed she'd see, the blue Atlantic was the same.

I still think the Pavilion's Moorish domes are a monstrosity.

They were painted a gaudy green that clashed with the grass of the surrounding lawn. Ena said the domes are painted a different color every year or two. But step inside, and the difference between Prinny's Pavilion and the over-stuffed stately homes and palaces I'd seen is extraordinary. No dark mahogany rooms smothered in heavy furniture, no massive oil paintings cramming every wall. The Pavilion is all uncluttered grace and light.

In the state drawing room, for instance, the cream-colored walls are decorated with only an occasional mirror bordered in thin gold. There are water-green satin drapes at the long windows, curved chairs covered in the same green satin, and green satin settees with thin gold-leaf borders in small alcoves under white arches.

We went into a second drawing room with bare white walls intersected by gold-leaf panels, and here and there Chinese stands painted in delicate patterns of lavender and rose, holding five-pronged candelabra. All the state rooms have the same uncluttered simplicity — in spite of the appalling amounts of money Prinny spent on them. (Upstairs, Queen Caroline's bedroom positively jumps with chinoiserie. Her taste in furnishings was fussier than her husband's.)

According to the booklets, it's because he spent so much money on architecture and palace interiors that Prinny has been an unpopular monarch for 250 years. He spent fortunes on palaces and parks at a time when England needed all the money it could raise to finance the Napoleonic War.

Well, the Napoleonic War was followed by the Crimean War and the Boer War and the First World War and the Second World War and they're all long gone.

The Pavilion at Brighton and Windsor Castle and Regent Street and Carlton House Terrace and Regent's Park and the Nash Terraces are all still here. Blessings on your farsighted spendthrift head, Prinny.

Thursday, August 10

A young reporter came to interview me this afternoon. She'd never been in a flat in St. John's Wood before so I showed her all of it and explained my absentee hostess was André's eighty-eight-year-old mother. I'd made coffee for us and I said:

"Do you mind if we have coffee and the interview in the kitchen instead of the living room? It's so far down the hall I got tired of running back and forth to hot up the coffee so now I never leave the kitchen."

"I'm sure Mrs. Deutsch has all her meals in the kitchen," she said. "She's probably not able to carry heavy trays down the hall."

"She doesn't know how lucky she is to have a kitchen big enough for a table and chairs," I said. "I wish I did."

"Well, you wouldn't be willing to put your refrigerator out in the hall to make room for it," she said.

Oh.

Friday, August 11

"Mr. Bernard Shaw regrets he cannot answer mail or acknowledge books sent to him because if he did, he wouldn't get any work done." But he thanks the sender . . .

The form letter is framed on a wall in Shaw's house at Ayot St. Lawrence and when I read it I thought it was the perfect solution to fan mail. Then I saw the catch. The letter only saves time for an author who can afford a secretary to read the mail, have copies of the form letter made, insert the letters in envelopes and address, seal, stamp and mail them.

Even if I had the money I couldn't answer fan mail with a mimeographed or Xeroxed form letter. But then, I feel very popular when I get ten or twelve letters a week. Shaw got 200 a *day*. For thirty or forty years.

Ena drove me down and there were "Shaw's Corner" signs all along the way. They're needed, because the house is in a woods, hidden both from the road and from the few neighboring houses. Being a big-city dweller, I couldn't live there all year round but neither did Shaw till he was very old. He was still writing to Ellen Terry from a London flat in 1938 and he was past eighty then.

Charlotte, his "green-eyed millionairess," obviously shared her husband's plain taste. The furnishings are those of any modest country house. Then you look at the framed photos on the mantel and you know this is not any modest country house. The framed photos are of Lenin, Ibsen, Stalin, Yeats and O'Casey.

There's a portrait of Charlotte above the mantel. There were no photos of Ellen Terry and Mrs. Pat Campbell. I thought Shaw might have put them on the mantel after Charlotte died. Then I read the Ayot booklet. It said that after Charlotte died Shaw kept her ashes for the seven years he outlived her, and left instructions that when he died his ashes were to be commingled with hers and scattered over the garden.

I don't know how many writers were contemptuous of that marriage because it was sexless. Edmund Wilson was one of them. How many wives did he have? Five?

"Let me not to the marriage of true minds admit impediment."

There's a study in the house, which is not where he worked. But there's a large desk in it — and even though it's obvious staging-for-tourists, Shaw's large china teacup and saucer and his gold-rimmed spectacles lying on the desk mesmerize you. It took all my willpower not to touch them.

There are wonderful cartoons of him on all the walls and a Rodin bust of him and a prankish marionette figure from the National Theatre's production of *Shaks. vs Shaw.* They borrow it back whenever they revive the play. And in a glass case, what must be a priceless possession: the prayer book of Charles I, printed a year before he was beheaded.

Then we left the house and walked down beyond the garden to his workroom, The Hut.

It's just that. One room, with a plain wooden desk, a

straight chair, a telephone and nothing else. You stand there, imagining him writing in perfect solitude and quiet — and then ruin the whole romantic image by remembering that Shaw wrote plays on clattery trains en route to speaking engagements on behalf of Socialist candidates or causes. He could write a play in bad light on a lurching, noisy train — in such clean, clear shorthand that when he got off the train with the final scene finished, he could mail his shorthand notebooks to his secretary in London knowing she'd have no trouble transcribing them, so that when he got home the play would be typed and ready for correction. He could write anywhere and under any conditions, and turn out a nearly perfect play in one draft and in less than one month.

I wish I knew who it was that corrected the old definition of genius.

"Talent," whoever-it-was said, "is the infinite capacity for taking pains. Genius is the infinite capacity for achievement without taking any pains at all."

It'll probably turn out the person who said it was Shaw.

Saturday, 12th

There's a little market across the street I never use since I love the High Street. But today I just needed coffee and eggs and I stopped in there. I was the only customer and when the owner saw me reach for my brand of coffee he got it down for me from a high shelf.

"Are you visiting in the neighborhood?" he asked.

"I'm staying across the street in Mrs. Deutsch's flat," I said.

"Oh, Mrs. Deutsch!" he said, pleased. "She used to buy Continental coffee, too. But these days she buys the Instant."

There was a big bin of eggs, several brands, so I said:

"Which eggs does she buy?"

"Oh, she won't buy my eggs!" he said, grinning. "She likes her eggs fresh from the hen! She has friends drive her out to a farm for them."

I came home, stopping in the kitchen to put the coffee away. I stared at the long mantel where nothing unsightly was allowed in plain view. And when I went into the bedroom, I saluted the empty egg cartons lined up on top of the mahogany wardrobe in the Spare Room, waiting for their next trip to the farm.

Sunday, August 13

Ena drove me to Cambridge along country roads, cows to the left of us, sheep to the right and a wild sky that looked as excited as I felt: bright blue with sunny white clouds, but above and behind them, huge grey-black storm clouds. Following Muriel Brittain's meticulous directions, Ena found Jesus College and the parking lot with no trouble. We started to climb Stairway No. 7, and were less than halfway up it when Muriel came running down to meet us. She's very small and light on her feet, with a light voice to match.

"We'd better go right in to lunch before the Hall closes," she said, and led the way into a large, long dining hall. It had a vaulted ceiling with immensely thick oak beams, and three dining tables that ran the length of the room, one along each side wall and one down the middle of the room, each with a long bench instead of chairs.

"It takes two sittings to feed the whole College at dinner," said Muriel.

Lunch was cafeteria-style and we got our trays and settled at a nearly empty table against one wall. At the front of the room, running the width of it, was the High Table for the "Fellows," and Muriel pointed to the two huge framed portraits on the wall above it. One was of Henry VIII, the other of Thomas Cranmer.

"Cranmer was an undergraduate at Jesus College a few years after it opened," she said. "And then he was elected a Fellow."

On the wall opposite was a portrait of an Archbishop of York who, said Muriel, was Laurence Sterne's great-grandfather. "They were both Jesus men."

"Laurence must have become a clergyman because it was the family profession," I said. "I've always had a theory that he got the idea for *Tristram Shandy* standing on the church steps greeting the members of the congregation as they filed out after Sunday services, and listening to their long-winded stories that kept wandering off on tangents and never got to the point."

Coleridge was also a Jesus man. I said I hadn't known that, and Muriel said, mildly exasperated:

"Well, he never finished, you know. He kept running away and coming back, and running away and coming back. Then he ran off to fight in the French Revolution and that was the end of it."

From her tone, you'd have thought it all happened last year.

You don't call Cambridge students "students," you call them "pupils" or "undergraduates."

I told her that at home "pupils" are grade-school children. As soon as they start high school they're students and they're "the student body" clear through college.

She informed us solemnly that the full name of the college is "The Ancient and Religious Foundation of the Blessed Virgin Mary, Saint John the Evangelist and the Glorious Virgin Saint Radegund, Commonly Called Jesus College." It was originally a Benedictine convent and its cloister dates back to the eleventh century. Saint Radegund lived in the sixth.

"She was the daughter of the King of Thuringia," said Muriel. "She was carried off by the Franks who married her forcibly to their King Clothair — a right bad lot who murdered her brother."

I forget how this made her a Glorious Virgin.

After lunch, Muriel walked up past a small alcove with a serving counter in front of it and said:

"This is where the nuns queued up for their daily ration of beer."

As we started up the staircase to Q's rooms I asked her the difference between a "don" and a "Fellow."

"At Cambridge," she said, "the teaching staff are dons. But a don has no college rooms of his own. He has to find lodgings in town until he's elected a Fellow by the Fellows of his College. Then he gets a home here, but only for himself. There are no rooms for his family."

"So all the years Q taught here, he had to leave his family in Cornwall," I explained to Ena. "He had a wife and a son and daughter. His son fought through World War I without being wounded, went to Berlin in 1918 with the Occupation Army, and in one weekend there, caught pneumonia and died."

At the top of the stairs, Muriel unlocked a door and

opened it and I followed her into Q's Common Room. His big armchair was in front of a grey stone fireplace. I heard Ena admiring the plum-colored damask wallpaper and mahogany furniture but I don't remember seeing them. I was finding a way around the furniture to get me closer to the photos of Q on the mantel.

"Your husband didn't say in his book how he came to know Q," I said.

"Freddy came up as an undergraduate in 1919," Muriel said. "Q sort of adopted him."

She must have been a generation younger than Freddy. He'd be in his eighties now; Muriel can't be out of her fifties.

She and Ena disappeared into the kitchen to make tea and I blessed them both for their tact in leaving me alone in the room for a few minutes. I went up to the mantel to look at the photos — there were several of him. It was a very kind face, weatherbeaten granite like the photo above his obituary notice in *The Times*. I imagined him lounging in his armchair with his students around him. They used to come there during the day as well as in the evening.

Muriel came in with the tea tray and Q's tobacco jar. Then she made me sit in his armchair for tea.

"I've read stories," I said, "about how much he resented women in his classes when they were first admitted to Jesus."

And Muriel said with energy:

"That's all nonsense, I don't know who started that story! He was as kind and generous to women undergraduates as he was to everybody else! And the women were all charmed by his passion for clothes. Did you know he changed his attire three times a day? He had ties to harmonize with all his bowlers. Here, I'll show you."

She went to a closet, rummaged in it and then held up a dashing green bowler and a matching tie. Then she brought me a dark brown bowler.

"This was his favorite," she said — and laid it in my lap.

It shocked me. Now that I knew he hadn't resented women students I felt less an intruder. I was shocked just the same, at sitting in his chair with his favorite hat in my hands. There was a kind of violation in being so familiar with his ghost.

And then I remembered something he'd said once, in a lecture. I don't remember what the subject of the lecture was, but he said he was offering his own view of it because "sometimes the clearest visions are those seen through the eyes of a friend." And he had added: "If that word be presumptuous, you must forgive me."

I'd loved him for that line when I first read it, because I was reading it in an edition printed expressly for American readers; knowing Q, I knew he'd edited it — and he'd let the line stand. If he saw himself as my friend I had a right to be there in his Common Room where his pupils had always been welcome.

Muriel took us through the rooms — the tiny kitchen, the bare, narrow bedroom as Spartan as a monastic cell. Most of his novels were about Fowey in Cornwall, where he lived, and looking at that monastic cell, I wondered if they'd been written out of homesickness during every year's long exile in Cambridge. But I think the exile was voluntary. He loved teaching.

We were there for three hours. By the time we left, I was convinced Q knew I was there and was pleased (and amused) that it meant so much to me.

-»» ««-

It was nearly five years later that a letter came one morning from a Londoner named Cecil Clarabut.

Dear Miss Hanff

Since he has meant so much to you I jot down a few memories of Q. He was the first professor of English Literature at Cambridge and was not lecturing very much when I arrived there, always without notes because of his poor eyesight. The style was the man: he spoke very much as he wrote, in a gentle and urbane manner.

He dressed often in tweeds, looking more like a countryman than a don. . . . He had a vast library which afterwards passed to the English department, situated in a block of lecture rooms known as the Divinity School opposite the entrance to St. John's, and it was a particular pleasure for a group of us reading for the honours course (tripos) to sit round a big fire and listen to him weekly as he smoked. Though he began as a Cornish writer, his power to evoke the Dorset atmosphere of Thomas Hardy made him seem a Wessexman and he made the brooding power of Egdon Heath unforgettable.

Years later I saw him last in retirement, walking in the cool of his garden at Fowey. . . .

FIVE

"Then to the well-trod stage anon . . ."

I OUT OF SIGHT, OUT OF MIND

THE LETTER FROM LONDON was addressed to Flora, my agent, and she read it to me over the phone, on a December day in 1980.

Dear Miss Roberts,

   I am interested in adapting the book '84, Charing Cross Road' for the stage, in both writing and directing it, though of course the words would be Ms. Hanff's . . .

James Roose-Evans

I told Flora to do whatever she thought best about the contract he proposed, and hung up and forgot about it. James Roose-Evans's letter lay outside my private universe, which, that December, contained nothing but Eyes. Cataracts had developed on both of mine. And since you may one day find yourself in the same situation, I pass on to you the two incontrovertible facts about it.

Fact One: Cataract surgery is simple, painless and (except with implants) risk-free; sight is easily restored by cataract spectacles, contact lenses or implants; the whole procedure is common, routine and nothing to worry about.

Fact Two: Fact One applies only to cataracts on the eyes in somebody else's head.

Never mind that when I took a bus down to Gene's 48th Street office on a rainy day, I had to get off at 57th Street, which I recognized by its width, and walk the remaining nine blocks in the rain, counting as I went, because I could no longer read street signs.

Never mind that at night I fell over curbstones I couldn't see, and down the fuzzy white stone steps at Lincoln Center — or that when I went Christmas shopping I fell down the blurred escalator steps at Saks and walked into a glass wall at Bloomingdale's. Never mind that marketing for Christmas dinner was a nightmare of blurred colors and fuzzy print on supermarket boxes, and price tags I couldn't read.

All of it was preferable to a surgeon's knife coming at my good right eye and maybe slipping when it got there. My left eye had always been nearly blind, I didn't worry about that one; but it made the right one indispensable. I was a writer, I lived alone and did my own cooking and housework. I could still see to type and when anybody asked when I was going to have my eyes operated on I said flatly:

"When I can no longer see to work."

In January, a charming letter arrived from James Roose-Evans to say he was hard at work on his adaptation of *84, Charing Cross Road,* which he hoped to produce at a summer theatre festival.

On a morning in February, I put paper in the typewriter, to answer a letter from André that lay alongside the typewriter. I glanced at the letter and saw, instead of typewritten lines, the dreaded blur. I got a magnifying glass and sweated out the answer. But Push had come to Shove. The next day I went shopping for an eye surgeon. I found one I trusted and set dates for two operations, the first on my half-blind left eye for the end of March, with the one on the right eye to follow at the end of April.

From the day I committed myself, I woke every morning promptly at five with an attack of panic and terror — euphemistically known as an Anxiety Attack — which lasted two hours. By March, the Anxiety Attacks were taking up most of the day.

That March, I got a phone call from Celeste Holm. Back in the *Oklahoma!* days, Celeste had been the easiest of all actresses for a timid press agent's assistant to interview. She was salty and pithy and down-to-earth and I liked her. Then she went to Hollywood and it was thirty years before I saw her again. In the mid-Seventies she'd phoned to say she wanted to give her father an autographed copy of *84* for Christmas, and would I have lunch with her? We met for lunch, and after thirty years of Hollywood stardom, she was still salty and pithy and down-to-earth.

Now she said on the phone, "I'm giving an *Oklahoma!* reunion. I'm inviting everybody who was connected in any way with any of the companies — three hundred so far. Are you good on your feet? Can you come and give a shorter version of the *Oklahoma!* story you told in *Underfoot in Show Business?*"

The reunion was to be held on March 31 — the anniversary of the show's opening — and I had to decline: I'd be in the hospital that day.

The nearly blind left eye was operated on successfully on March 30.

In April, a letter from James Roose-Evans announced that his adaptation of *84* was finished and that he hoped to produce it at the Salisbury summer theatre festival. I don't remember whether I answered him. James Roose-Evans's petty affairs couldn't compete with the panic that occupied all of April till the surgery on the thirtieth.

The operation was wildly successful. "Wildly" because I'd expected to wake up blind till I was given spectacles — and I didn't. Having been very nearsighted all my life, I discovered, when the patch came off my eye, that I could see as well as I'd ever seen without glasses. I woke up to the same fuzzy world I'd always seen. There was only one small hitch.

"You won't be able to read for a month," the surgeon warned me as we parted. "Come back in a month and I'll give you a prescription for glasses." He offered me temporary cataract spectacles to wear on the street, but I'd heard these were difficult to get used to and I knew I could manage without them. In a month I'd get permanent spectacles for both reading and distance wear.

I left the hospital and rode home in a friend's car in a state of blissful relief. I could live without reading for a month, surely? Surely. I got out of the car, floated into the lobby and was welcomed by the super and the doorman. Then I went into the mail room to pick up my mail.

The long rows of mailboxes were still there — but the boxes no longer had numbers on them. I called the doorman and he came and showed me which box had 8-G on it in invisible letters. I opened the box and took out of it a pile of blank envelopes. I carried them to the elevator, stepped into it and confronted a double row of buttons which no longer had floor numbers on them. I called the doorman again and he came and showed me which button said 8 and I memorized its position. By which time I was shaken enough to want to call my best friend, and as soon as I'd let myself into my apartment I hurried to the phone. But of course, the phone dial had no numbers on it. Neither did the clock. Neither did the radio.

"You won't be able to read . . ."

Friends and neighbors flocked to the rescue. My friend Lolly took a morning off from her insurance business every week to do my marketing and go through the mail, pulling out the doctors' bills and medical insurance forms, writing checks for me and showing me where to sign them in invisible ink. And not for the first time did a New York apartment house turn out to be a life-support system. Neighbors dialed the phone for me, set the oven for me, wrote checks to cash for me and took them to the bank and cashed them — and folded the dollar bills into separate piles so I'd know the ones from the tens.

Meanwhile, it was May — and I discovered I could see curbs and traffic lights clearly. I'd had months of practice at finding my way around town without being able to read signs by memorizing landmarks and I began walking all day long, through Central Park and all over town, without mishap if not exactly without incident.

There was, for instance, the beautiful brown-and-white collie who came toward me one day in the park and who, as I stooped to pet him, turned into a brown suitcase in a man's white-cuffed hand. And there was the lovely Saturday afternoon when I was sailing insouciantly down Fifth Avenue and saw ahead of me a large pink banner streaming down the familiar steps of St. Thomas's church. St. Thomas's has wonderful choral concerts and I hoped the banner was advertising one of them, as the crowd at the side of the steps seemed to indicate. The crowd blocked my way and I detoured around it and down to the curb — just as a limousine door opened and a misty white bride walked into me. That's when I saw that the large pink banner had turned into six pink bridesmaids lined up in formation on the church steps. I fled to the far side steps of the church, and, having no prior engagement, went to the wedding.

I couldn't bother friends and neighbors with any mail that didn't contain bills or checks and I ignored the growing unopened pile, including a large manila envelope. But June finally came and I went down to the surgeon's office, got prescriptions for cataract spectacles and carried them — all unsuspecting — to the optometrist. On the day I picked them up he said to me:

"You'll want to practice with these."

He was wrong. I never wanted to practice with them.

When I say that the first time you put on cataract spectacles they magnify everything and distort everything, I mean that when I put them on, my typewriter was instantly the size of an Alfa Romeo — and when I headed for the kitchen for the martini I suddenly needed, the kitchen door, big as a wall, curved menacingly outward toward me at a 90-degree angle.

I took the damned things off and made my martini without them. Then I scooped up the pile of mail, settled in the armchair, put the spectacles back on and reached for the large manila envelope. I took out of it James Roose-Evans's script of *84* and all I can tell you about it is that it was huge. I never knew the mere size of things could be so intimidating. When I turned toward the ceramic ashtray at my elbow, it had become a great vat and I shrank from it.

A couple of nights later I tried wearing the Fun House mirrors on the street and promptly fell over a curb that looked two feet closer than it was. I was also nearly hit by a cab zooming around a corner I couldn't see, because cataract spectacles give you "no peripheral vision," a smooth phrase meaning that if you look sideways out of them you fall off the edge of the world.

Somebody told me that contact lenses didn't distort and magnify the world and the minute I heard this, I phoned my surgeon.

"I want contact lenses," I said.

"Good! Fine!" he said. "Come back in two months when your eyes have healed."

In July, James Roose-Evans wrote to say that *84* would open in Salisbury in August. Was I coming over for it? No, I wasn't. The letter might have come from some other planet for all it had to do with me.

In August, the surgeon pronounced my eyes healed and sent me across the hall to Dr. Siegel, the lens expert. He inserted soft contact lenses in both eyes and the miracle happened: the world was instantly bright and clear and of normal size again. And I had enough peripheral vision to protect me from berserk New York cab drivers.

However:

Soft contact lenses are tiny, almost invisible rounds of plastic, and you position one on the tip of your index finger and insert it deftly in your eye. You insert it deftly in your eye if you're deft. If you're not — I am not — you stand at the bathroom sink and, wearing the Fun House mirrors, position the tiny round of plastic on the tip of your index finger. You remove the spectacles and raise your index finger toward your eye — whereupon the lens flies off it, into the Great Beyond. You don't know whether it flew upward and landed on the top of the shower curtain, or downward to lodge somewhere in your shaggy bathroom carpet. You put on your cataract spectacles and turn the bathroom upside down and you don't find it. Three days later you may find a dried speck of something under the doorstop but when you put it in lens fluid to soften you discover that what you found isn't a lens, it's half-a-lens.

I lost eight in the first month. Two a week, regular as clockwork. There was a ninth that I can't properly call Lost since I know where it is. My bathroom was freshly painted at the end of August and one morning as I lifted my index finger to my eye, the lens flew off it and landed on the wall behind me where it attached itself to the sticky white enamel. (It's still there. It gleams at me on Saturday mornings when I'm cleaning the bathroom and wipe down the wall. When I'm feeling pleasant I say hello to it.)

Plus Which. (And I really felt sorry for Dr. Siegel, a man of infinite patience, good humor and optimism, because as time went on the Plus Which wore even him out.)

The day he first put the lenses in for me, he asked me how they felt.

"Wonderful," I said, "except the right one feels as if it's going to drop out."

"That," said Dr. Siegel, "doesn't happen."

We left his First Avenue office together. He was going

on vacation, I was going to walk over to Fifth Avenue, to shop for the first time in six months. I got as far as Madison and was halfway across it when the right lens dropped out on my cheek. I couldn't see if, of course; I could only feel it. Clutching it between thumb and forefinger, I hailed a cab and went home and (in not much more than a couple of hours) put it back in.

From then on, the right lens dropped out two or three times a day. I phoned Dr. Siegel's assistant, who said conversationally:

"Your eye appears to be rejecting the lens."

In extremis, I called Bud, my personal doctor, and wept into his sympathetic ear.

"A lot of my patients have eyes that rejected the lens at first," said Bud. "The lens is a foreign substance and the eye wants to be rid of it. But if you insist, your eye will finally accept it. Okay?"

Okay. I mapped out a program for Insisting. I was fairly good at self-hypnosis and I'd read an article about biofeedback. I began hypnotizing myself and giving my right eye biofeedback instructions under hypnosis:

"The lens is not a foreign substance, it is a houseguest! It is there to *help* you! You will regard it as a FRIEND!"

My right eye listened to this spiel three times a day for half an hour each time and went right on throwing the lens out — in the bank, on somebody's terrace, at the supermarket checkout counter.

By September, the wonderful reviews of *84* sent to me by James Roose-Evans from Salisbury meant far less to me than the new technique a friend taught me for inserting the lenses. (It's the mountain-to-Mohammed technique: You don't lift your finger to your eye, you lower your eye to your finger.) I began putting them in without losing them — with the aid of reminder signs Scotch-taped to the bathroom wall:

STOPPER IN SINK.

JOHN LID *DOWN!*

STAND PRESSED AGAINST SINK SO LENS
DROPS *IN* IT.

When I found that last one in a desk drawer months later, STAND had been crossed out and SIT substituted, with the word CHAIR printed at the bottom in case I didn't know what SIT meant.

In September, André Deutsch came to breakfast and said briskly:

"Darling, I want you to write me a short, funny book about cataracts." He was lucky I didn't throw him out the eighth-floor window.

In October, James Roose-Evans wrote to say that he had sold *84, Charing Cross Road* to a London West End producer named Michael Redington. I wrote and congratulated him, and went on trying to hypnotize my right lens, which went on dropping out.

Early in November, Sheila Murphy phoned. Sheila was André's press agent.

"Michael Redington," she said, "is opening *84, Charing Cross Road* at the Ambassadors Theatre on Thursday, 26 November. He wants to bring you to London for a week before the opening to publicize the show. He'll pay all expenses. Isn't that lovely?"

I had visions of the right lens dropping into oblivion in Heathrow Airport and the spare lens dropping out on the sidewalk the next day, leaving me at the mercy of the Fun House spectacles for the rest of the week. I opened my date book to November 26 and saw my excuse.

"I can't come," I said. "November 26 is Thanksgiving Day. It's a big holiday, I have commitments here on Thanksgiving."

"Michael will be so disappointed," said Sheila. "He's so anxious to have you come! Will you think about it?"

I said I'd think about it and we hung up. My friend Richard was having coffee with me at the time, and since he's one of the friends who come here to Thanksgiving dinner I explained the conversation to him. Richard is a laconic man and usually imperturbable but he stared at me in disbelief.

"After all the years you spent trying to crash the theatre as a playwright," he said, "somebody's made a play from your book, it's opening in the West End — and you're not going to the Opening?" And he added drily: "Your 'commitments' will have you committed if you don't go."

And I think that's when it finally dawned on me that what James Roose-Evans had been slaving over, all these months, had something to do with me.

"I have to go, don't I?" I said.

But I lay awake a long time that night dreading the trip, and when Sheila Murphy phoned the next day she had to cope with a cranky five-year-old who after much pleading, says All right, she'll Go to the dentist, but she has to wear her pink dress and she has to take her doll along and she has to have ice cream afterward and they can't take it home, she has to have it in the ice-cream parlor.

"Michael," said Sheila, opening negotiations, "will put you up at any hotel you name."

"I don't care what hotel it is, but it has to be a good one, I'm sick of cheap hotels," I said. "And it has to be in

Marylebone. If I'm coming to London for a raw November week, at least I'm going to be in the neighborhood I like best." (I didn't think there were any hotels in Marylebone; it's residential.) "If he can't find a good hotel in Marylebone I'm not coming."

"He'll find one," said Sheila.

"And I'm not taking a night flight where you walk around like a zombie with jet-lag for two days," I said. "There's only one day flight I know of, it's B.A. If he can't get me on that I'm not coming."

"If he can't get you on that," said Sheila tranquilly, "he'll fly you Concorde."

So then of course I prayed the B.A. flight would be sold out. But God doesn't hear greedy prayers and Sheila phoned back a day later to say I was booked on B.A.'s 10 a.m. flight for Wednesday, November 18.

"You're at the St. Georges Hotel," she said. "I went around to see it and it's lovely. It's in Marylebone."

That afternoon an enormous bouquet arrived. From Michael Redington — to thank me for letting him give me a free trip to London. And the five-year-old cabled graciously:

THANKS FOR BEAUTIFUL FLOWERS TELL BA MUST HAVE WINDOW SEAT IN SMOKING SECTION

Sheila phoned the next day to report:

"B.A. has reserved you a window seat in the smoking section." Then she said: "Leo and Ena Marks have money in the show. And André Deutsch Ltd. has money in it." And she added in a voice heavily casual, "I'll have you know the Press Department has fifty quid in it."

Suddenly I had tears in my eyes.

On the Sunday before I was to leave for London the right lens dropped out in a box at Lincoln Center. On Monday I turned up in Dr. Siegel's office and said Do Something.

He sat me down at a little machine and peered into my eyes through a magnifying glass.

"Oh, that's interesting!" he said. "I can see the stitches! Tissue has grown over them in your left eye — but they're visible in your right eye and they're pushing the lens around!"

And he sent me across the hall to the surgeon's office. The surgeon sat me down at another machine with my chin on a metal chin-rest and my eyes in little metal frames, and examined my right eye. Then he picked up a little scissors. As his hand with the scissors in it came straight at the naked eyeball of the only eye I see with, he said in a measured doomlike monotone:

"Don't — — Move"

and I sat frozen while he snipped ten or twelve stitches out of my eye. I left that office bathed in sweat but so full of joyful relief that in spite of the raw November wind I started walking the forty blocks home.

"Well, of *course* the lens dropped out on your way home!" said my friend Nina in her positive way, as I came weeping into the lobby. "Your eye is puffy from the irritation of having the stitches taken out! The puffiness will be gone in a day or two and it'll never drop out again!"

She was right. Though it would be a month before I dared to believe it, the nightmare was finally over.

On Tuesday night I packed a suitcase with my best clothes and my two prized possessions: an extra pair of contact lenses, and the miserable cataract spectacles without which I couldn't see to clean the lenses or position them on my index finger. The strange thing about the spectacles was that sometimes, when my eyes felt gritty at the end of a long day, I found myself taking out the lenses an hour before I went to bed and wearing the specs to watch the late-night TV news. And when I went out to the kitchen to wash the coffee pot or get a glass of milk, the kitchen door no longer curved menacingly outward. The spectacles had adjusted to me.

On Wednesday morning, I took the plane to London.

II CENTER STAGE

Dieter, a Deutsch editor, met me at Heathrow and drove me to the St. Georges, but it was too dark and rainy for me to see where it was. We had drinks in an attractive top-floor restaurant, then Dieter left and I took the elevator down to my room, turned the key in the lock and — appropriately for Cinderella — at exactly midnight walked in. From that moment, the trip had a dreamlike unreality it never lost.

I wasn't in a hotel room, I was in the living room of a suite, with a deep sofa and armchairs, a bar-stocked refrigerator in one corner and a color TV set in the other. There were bouquets with cards stuck in them, on the coffee-table and both end tables, there were letters and greeting cards propped up on the mantel, there was a supper tray of cold meats and salads protected under plastic on the coffee-table in front of the sofa.

My suitcase had been deposited in the bedroom and when I went in there to unpack, I saw beyond it a dressing room — its long dressing table fitted with two small sinks, two bright table lamps and two tufted chairs, expressly designed for guests with contact lenses and ten thumbs.

I unpacked, had a leisurely bath, put on a robe, sashayed in to supper and read the cards and letters as I ate. The card in the most breathtaking bouquet — an enormous profusion of buds and flowers — was from Michael Redington and said he hoped to see me at the theatre at four on Thursday. There was a note from Ena to say she'd call me in the morning, and a note from Abbe enclosing press clippings about the show:

"Elizabeth Taylor's in town for her opening but you and *84* are getting much more publicity. Liz, eat your heart out."

There was a letter from James Roose-Evans to say he was giving a luncheon for me at the Garrick Club on Sunday. There was a letter from Sue Hyman, the show's press agent, with two typewritten pages of interview dates attached. And I hadn't even brought a notebook to use as a date book.

Lying next to the supper tray was a copy of the Celebrity Bulletin. I hadn't seen one of those since the Theatre Guild days. I ran my eye down the alphabetical list of Who Was In Town This Week — and the two names, one after the other, jumped out at me:

Helene Hanff
Celeste Holm

"Lookit that, I'm a celebrity," I thought. Celeste wasn't in London, she was in Nottingham rehearsing *Lady in the Dark*. I had a sudden urge to phone the number given in the Bulletin — till I realized it was one-thirty a.m. I finished my coffee and floated off to bed.

After breakfast the next morning — in style, in the living

room — I thought I'd better buy a notebook-datebook before the first interviewer arrived. I went down to the lobby, walked out to the sidewalk — and stood and stared. I was standing on the corner with the London view I loved best. The St. Georges was at the top of Regent Street, looking up the wide avenue of Portland Place to the Nash crescents flanking the entrance to Regent's Park. They beckoned in the misty rain and I walked out to them — and then had to run all the way back to Mortimer Street to pick up a notebook, getting back up the suite two minutes before the first interviewer arrived.

They came all morning, with just time for a late lunch before Sue Hyman arrived at three. She was a pretty woman in her thirties, a wife and mother and head of her own P.R. firm, and awesomely efficient.

"A car will be here to take you to Thames Television at eleven. A car will be waiting there for you at twelve to take you to . . ."

I wasn't even allowed to walk down Regent Street to the Ambassadors Theatre five minutes away on foot. "A car will be here . . ."

It was, and it dropped me in front of a theatre plastered with posters advertising the show. With my name on them in big block letters. Thirty years after I'd given up trying to write plays, my name on those posters was too far-fetched to be real. It was just part of the dream I was living in.

Michael Redington was waiting for me in the lobby and he drove me home to his house in Westminster for tea.

Michael is one of those rare gentle men to whom the word "sweet" applies. He was lean and sandy-haired and he must have been in his late fifties ("I was company manager for the Lunts when they toured Australia in the Forties," he told me), but he looked younger; maybe because after working in the theatre all his life, he was still stage-struck, he still had a youthful enthusiasm about it. He'd been a company manager and press agent for years; he was now finally a producer and when he said, "*84* is my first West End production!" you could hear the exclamation point.

I told him his flowers were dazzling and he said:

"Ann, my wife, is a florist. She plans a bouquet so that when the flowers blooming today begin to die, a group of buds will be just ready to open. One variety won't open till your last day."

He spent an hour — he could have spent six — showing me his collection of theatre photos and programs, and he gave me one of his favorite theatre books to take home. It's called *Time Was;* it's the memoirs of a costumer and set-designer named Graham Robertson who worked in the London theatre of Ellen Terry and Henry Irving, Sarah Bernhardt and Oscar Wilde, and I love it.

There was a lunch interview on my schedule for Friday and the name of the interviewer conjured up a memory of my first morning in London ten years before. I'd gone up the street from the hotel to André Deutsch's office to be interviewed by "a bouncy young reporter from the *Evening Standard* named Valerie Jenkins," it said in my diary. Since then, Valerie had become one of the best-known newspaper columnists in a city that still published eight daily newspapers. She was listed on the schedule as "Valerie Jenkins (Grove)." When she arrived, she seemed as young and bouncy as ever, though she told me she and her husband — a fellow newspaper writer — had three daughters.

She drove me out to a North London restaurant near where she lived, and as we finished lunch she said:

"Do you mind driving back to the house with me? Lesley, my mother-in-law, wants to meet you."

And I call blessings down on Lesley's attractive head because if she hadn't wanted to meet me, I would never have got to see that house. To walk into Valerie's house is to walk back into another time and another world.

We met Lesley in the sitting room — big and old-fashioned with small sofas and armchairs in bright flowered slipcovers and a massive fireplace at one end. Then Lesley and Valerie took me on a tour of the house. There was a library cheerful with white bookshelves and a water-green carpet; a big dining room with knotty pine table and chairs, a red brick fireplace and hand-painted plates in immaculate rows above the mantel; and a children's sitting room — "the day nursery," said Lesley, as if Queen Victoria weren't dead — with child-sized table and chairs, including a child-sized rocker, William Morris wallpaper and old-fashioned toys: alphabet blocks, toy animals, a rocking horse.

But it was the levels of the house that gave it its nineteenth-century flavor. You go down half a flight from the sitting room to the "day nursery" and down another half flight to the kitchen and dining room. You go up half a flight to the guest bedroom, up another half to the master bedroom, a third to the "night nursery" and a fourth to Lucy's room. ("Lucy, being six," explained Valerie, "decided she was too old for the night nursery.") At the top of the house were two large bed-sitters — one in green and white for Lesley when she visits, the other in pink and white for Nanny.

Because of the levels, the house was full of small landings and hidden nooks for playing hide-and-seek on a rainy day. And of course there was a back garden, and of course

Nanny and the two smaller children had gone walking, accompanied by the family dog. They came back just as I was leaving — and Nanny confounded all my notions of nannies by being twenty-two and very pretty.

The aura of that house — the sense of a bygone security that conjured up Louisa May Alcott's world — was to stay with me for months. So was the astonishment that it had been created by parents who were 1980s newspaper reporters. Their breakfast and dinner conversations aren't calculated to shield their children from the modern world. They just don't let the modern world rob childhood of its birth rights.

On Saturday, Abbe phoned and I told her to come to the hotel and have dinner with me on Sunday night.

"Phone before you come to make sure I'm back," I said. "James Roose-Evans is giving a luncheon for me at the Garrick Club and I don't know how late I'll be there."

"Oh, Gawd!" said Abbe. "The Garrick is the most prestigious theatre club in London! Only the best names are elected to it — and no one can set foot in it who's not a member or guest of a member."

Michael drove me to the club, in the heart of the theatre district, and sure enough, when he opened the imposing front door, a doorman loomed up instantly, barring the way for all his courteous "Good morning."

"We're guests of Mr. James Roose-Evans," said Michael. And the doorman stood aside, gestured toward a grand staircase and said:

"They're in the Morning Room. Go right up."

We crossed a wide foyer and began to climb the broad mahogany stairs, stopping now and then to look at the wall alongside us, with its massively framed portraits of legendary London stage stars, painted in the costumes of their most famous roles, some against the backdrop of the stage sets used in their grandest scenes.

The floor above opened into a museum hall filled with glass cases of theatrical memorabilia. I yearned to stop and examine everything in every case, but Michael led the way past them and into the Morning Room. It was a large, comfortable clubroom with easy chairs grouped around small tables. The walls of the room were crammed with more framed oil portraits of theatre celebrities, the narrow spaces between them filled with miniature portraits.

Michael led the way to a small group having drinks at a table by the long windows, and a big, benign-looking man with a middle-aged bespectacled face rose and held out both hands to me and introduced himself as James Roose-Evans.

I discovered over lunch that he was the founder of the Hampstead Theatre (the best and oldest Fringe theatre in London), the author of several books about the theatre and several TV documentaries for the BBC — and that he writes a popular series of children's books published by André Deutsch. (I labor mightily to bring forth a mouse of a book and I can't do anything else whatever.)

I sat next to Rosemary Leach, who was playing me in *84*, and across from David Swift, who was playing Frank Doel. Rosemary, a friendly outgoing soul who told me all about her actor husband and Mrs. Brains, the family dog, is a big TV star in London.

"I've been acting in television for so long I can't believe I'm back in the theatre."

We moved next door to the dining room for lunch. If there were famous faces lunching there, I didn't recognize them. But there was a face at the center of one table that drew me like a magnet. It belonged to an elderly *grande dame* who was holding court at a table of younger admirers. Her beautiful white hair was framed by a black velvet hat — gently out of date and the only hat in the room — and in its discreet and expert makeup her face looked serenely unlined. Her flowing print dress, like the hat, was deliberately out of fashion; it told you she preferred Yesterday. I've never seen anyone who had so perfected the art of combining old age and glamour.

Rosemary had never been in the Garrick Club before and we both wanted to look at those glass cases, so when lunch ended she asked James:

"Will it be all right if Helene and I stay and look at all the things out in the hall?"

— and James told us expansively to tour the building and stay as long as we liked. The others left and the two of us started slowly along the cases in the museum hall, examining every glamorous item.

There was a cast of Duse's hand and a printed invitation to Bernhardt's funeral. There was a fan used on stage by Helena Modesta, Macready's stage garter worn in *Richard III,* a dog collar that had been worn by Edmund Kean's St. Bernard, and Henry Irving's dog whistle. And Irving's powder box, "Donated by Michael Redgrave." And Charles Kean's shoe buckle and George Arliss's walking stick and Ivor Novello's cigarette case. And a walking stick thought to have belonged to David Garrick himself, "Donated by Mr. Lunt, U.S.A." Near the glass cases on a small stand was a bust of John Gielgud and on the wall above it a miniature portrait of Garrick "made of the spun hair of Mr. and Mrs. Garrick." And on a stand, a polished goblet that Garrick had had made for a fellow actor, from the wood of the mulberry tree in Shakespeare's garden.

We climbed another flight of stairs, the walls alongside

lined with older paintings, and found on the top floor two dark, musty rooms, one full of faded portraits of long-forgotten stars, the other a library, its heavy brown shelves and tables piled high with three centuries of books on the theatre, in all sizes and shapes, some covered in faded silk, some in age-stained white vellum, some in thin leather so old and frail we were afraid to touch it.

As we left the club, Rosemary told me the cast was rehearsing all day every day and giving a preview performance every evening. Previews tell the director what scenes work and what ones don't, and he makes changes accordingly, but the changes can frazzle an actress.

"Before the preview Friday night, James told me the John Donne letter was being taken out," Rosemary said. "But when I got to rehearsal on Saturday morning, they'd changed their minds and the John Donne letter was back in. I don't know whether it'll be in or out tomorrow night."

I told her I was avoiding the previews. I wanted to see the show fresh on Opening Night.

On Monday morning, the interviewing began to get out of hand. I was sitting down to my breakfast eggs when the phone rang and a man at the other end said:

"This is the Sunday *Express*. We'd like to interview you."

"Fine," I said, and was reaching for my date book when he began to interview me then and there while my eggs got cold. We hung up and I finished the eggs and was pouring my coffee when the phone rang again and a woman said:

"This is the *Express*. We'd like to interview you."

"Somebody from the *Express* just did," I said.

"That was the Sunday *Express*. This is the Daily," she said — and interviewed me for fifteen minutes while my coffee got cold. I carried the coffee pot to the bedroom and was just pouring the coffee into the electric teakettle when the doorbell rang, announcing the first (scheduled) interviewer of the day.

On Tuesday, there was a company lunch at Futura, the paperback house. But Futura had been bought by MacDonald since my last lunch there, and when I walked into the office, all the '78 Upwardly Mobiles were gone, replaced by an entirely new set. The new ones were more relaxed and — sign of the times — there were young female faces sprinkled among the buttoned-down males.

What happened on Wednesday was so beyond imagining I have difficulty believing it even now. Ena came at noon to drive me to the remodeled building on Charing Cross Road that had once housed Marks & Co.'s bookshop. The small stone pillars that had flanked the shop's front door were still there, but they no longer bore the numbers 84. The old store had been split into two small stores. Both were new, unoccupied and unnumbered.

There was a small cluster of people gathered on the sidewalk. Abbe (who lived across the street) was there, and Leo Marks and Michael Redington, and André and half his staff, including Sheila Murphy, who informed me:

"We're the Rent-a-crowd."

I was introduced to a bearded young man from the real estate firm that had remodeled the building, and he led me to the left-hand stone pillar. There was a small curtain on it with a drawstring. Two photographers were standing near it. One of them showed me where to stand and the other told me when to pull the drawstring. I pulled it and the curtain rolled aside, exposing a round brass plaque. On it, in neat block letters, was the inscription:

84
CHARING CROSS ROAD
THE BOOKSELLERS MARKS & CO.
WERE ON THIS SITE WHICH
BECAME WORLD RENOWNED
THROUGH THE BOOK BY
HELENE HANFF

Press agents and photographers were issuing instructions and in a fog, I moved where they told me to move and posed for pictures and didn't know I was posing with Leo, son-of-Marks-&-Co., with André, then with the bearded young man from the real estate office, until weeks later when the photos came in the mail.

I knew perfectly well that the plaque had been put up by the real estate firm as a sop to the neighborhood, which had fought a long, losing battle to save the old Charing Cross Road bookshops. Of course the realtors had had to get approval of the plaque from the London City Council, but I knew that real estate developers always had political connections. None of it mattered. Whatever the motives behind it, there was a plaque on a London wall with my name on it. Through more posed photographs I stared at the fact of it and couldn't make myself believe it.

The realtors had a lunch for us after the ceremony and as we walked toward the restaurant Michael told me:

"André will be sitting with you tomorrow night. You're on the second row."

It horrified me.

"Oh, please don't trap me down front where Rosemary can't help seeing me!" I said. "Can't I hang over the back rail, so I can flee to the lobby if I need to?"

"There is no back rail," said Michael. "The theatre has graduated tiers rising to the last row of the balcony. I'll put you in a box where there's an exit."

It was five-thirty when I got back to the hotel on Thursday afternoon. The Opening Night curtain was to go up at seven and the theatre was only a few minutes' drive from the hotel. But knowing the perils of the telephone, I buzzed my friend the operator.

"Honey, do me a favor and don't put any calls through for the next hour," I said. "I have to bathe and dress and I want to take my time."

"There's a call for you now," she said. "It's the last one I'll put through."

It was Sheila calling.

"André will pick you up in a cab at six," she said.

Six?

"Sheila," I said. "We could walk to the theatre in five minutes! Tell him six-thirty."

"He doesn't want to be late," said Sheila.

"Just tell him I can't be ready before six-thirty," I said and hung up.

I got out my black velvet pantsuit and white blouse and then debated whether to wear the new shoes that hurt, or my old black velvet scuffs, as comfortable as old bedroom slippers and just as shabby. I decided to wear the new shoes and carry the scuffs in a Fortnum's shopping bag.

This weighty question settled, I ran a tub and had one foot in it when the phone rang. I went into the bedroom and picked it up.

"What happened?" I said to the operator.

"I'm sorry," she said, her voice awed, "It's Celeste Holm calling from Nottingham!"

Celeste was calling to wish me luck on the Opening.

At 6:15 the desk phoned to say Mr. Deutsch was in the lobby. I made him wait five minutes and even so, we got to the theatre before 6:30. There was a crowd in the lobby and it seemed to me hundreds of people had turned and were staring fixedly at me. It made me nervous and I murmured to André:

"Why are they looking at me?"

"They recognize you," he said. "They've seen your picture in the newspapers all week and they've seen you on television."

Not having seen the interviews, I hadn't realized Sue Hyman's press agentry had made my face a household item.

We went upstairs to the bar — and all the way up, we were waylaid by theatregoers who thrust programs at me to be signed. André brought me a martini but didn't let me finish it; he was convinced that if we didn't get to our seats fifteen minutes before the curtain it would rise without us. Till he led the way to it, it hadn't occurred to me that André felt obliged to sit with me in the upper box, where he couldn't see Rosemary's half of the stage at all. I've felt guilty about that ever since.

At a little after seven, the houselights dimmed and the curtain went up to reveal a split stage, with an old, shabby secondhand bookshop on the right and an equally shabby bed-sitter on the left. And I heard Rosemary's friendly voice read the date of the first letter:

"October 5, 1949."

I'm not sure when it started, but the curtain hadn't been up very long when I began to hear sniffles in the audience. It startled me.

There was nothing in the least sad taking place on stage. What was going on was a perfectly cheerful transatlantic conversation. It took me a little time to realize that something profoundly different was going on, in the minds of the people around me. They were caught up in a wave of nostalgia. They were carried back to bombed-out postwar London, to the grey years of food shortages when the arrival of a food parcel from America was a red-letter event in their rationed lives. As the evening wore on, everybody in the audience was reliving the sad funeral of King George VI and the high hopeful day of the young Queen's coronation. Everybody, that is, but the lone American sitting dry-eyed and restive in an upper box.

I was gratefully aware that Rosemary was reading my letters with extraordinary warmth, wit and comprehension. But I'd read those letters in Hugh Whitemore's TV script and heard them read over and over, every day for ten long days of rehearsal; I'd had to read them again, in scripts submitted for my approval by amateur theatre groups from Massachusetts to Hong Kong; I'd had to read James's script before it opened in Salisbury and again after he'd made changes in it for London. Now, at the Opening Night in London when I most wanted to relive the correspondence for my own personal reasons, I was finally sick to death of it.

After intermission Michael moved me to an empty seat in the upper balcony.

"We want you to take a curtain call with the cast and it will be easier to lead you down from here," he said.

At the final curtain, the audience erupted in the kind of applause you hear only at the opening of a hit. Michael came for me and led me down the narrow balcony stairs to the mezzanine, on down to the orchestra floor and then along the side aisle to the far end where a door led around a corner to the backstage area. When we got there the applause and the curtain calls were still going on.

Somebody took my arm and pointed to a door through which I was to walk onto the stage. I didn't know, till I read it in one of the reviews, that I was walking onstage through the door of my bookshop. Rosemary and David separated to make room for me between them and I stood blinking in the white glare of the footlights at the total blackness which was all I could see beyond. When the curtain finally came down to stay, the cast gave me a leather-bound copy of *84* with the complete cast list printed in it and their signatures alongside their names.

Gene Young and Little, Brown had presented me with a leather-bound copy of *Underfoot in Show Business* when it was reissued, and I never told her how it shocked me. I have my own standard of what books belong in fine leather covers and what ones don't. But the leather-bound *84* seemed to me then, and seems to me now, a fitting memorial to Marks & Co. and Frank Doel and all their vanished kind; and for their sakes I treasure it.

We assembled in the lobby — Leo and Ena, Michael and Ann Redington and James and I. (André had gone home; he was leaving early the next morning on a skiing vacation.)

We were going to walk around the corner to the Opening Night party being held in the empty storefront at what had been 84, Charing Cross Road. But we were waylaid in the lobby by half the audience who knew one or another of us. The first familiar faces I saw belonged to Sheila and Mary Doel, accompanied by their husbands and the ghosts of their parents (Nora had died the year before). After that, it seemed to me every soul I'd ever met in London came up to congratulate me. Michael and James had far more friends to deal with, and it was an hour before we finally got out of the theatre.

We were only going around the corner, but the new shoes declined to walk that far. I stopped on the sidewalk, took them off, put on the scuffs, and gave the shoes to Leo to put in his overcoat pockets. I figured nobody at the party would be staring at my feet. As it turned out, nobody at that party could see anybody's feet.

The empty storefront was absolutely bare. There wasn't a table or a folding chair in it. The party had been in full swing for an hour and the room was wall-to-wall people. There must have been a bar at the other end because everybody had a glass in hand, but I never got far enough into the room to see the other end. Five feet inside the entrance I was stopped by a solid phalanx of tuxedos and evening gowns that somehow kept moving without going any-where. People I knew and people I didn't know came up to congratulate me and somebody put a martini in my hand. In five minutes I'd lost sight of Ena and Leo, Ann and Michael and James. Ten more minutes and the sea of bodies had backed me into a corner between two walls.

It was after ten. I'd had nothing to eat since a hurried

sandwich at noon, I was tired and hungry and I don't like big parties anyway.

"The hell with it," I thought, and sat down on the bare floor and leaned back against the wall to finish my martini and think my thoughts. As I turned to put down my empty glass, I saw — lined up against the wall beside me in a neat row — four more martinis brought to me, I assume, by four separate well-wishers. I had doubts about the wisdom of another martini on my very empty stomach, but I picked up one of them — whereupon a passing male foot bumped into my hand, spilling half the martini on my right scuff. While I was mopping it up with tissue, a gentleman loomed above me, leaned down and said solicitously:

"Can I get you anything?"

"Yes," I said. "Leo Marks."

The gentleman went off and a few minutes later Leo appeared at the edge of the human sea and said:

"Yes, love?"

And I said simply:

"Get me out of here."

And Leo, his baritone deepening at the crisis, said:

"Instantly, my darling!"

and plunged back into the mob. Then miraculously Ena appeared at my elbow.

"Leo's gone for the car," she said. We went to dinner and they drove me home, and by midnight I was crawling thankfully into bed.

Back in the days when New York, too, had eight daily newspapers, theatre people stayed up till four a.m. for the morning reviews and then went to bed and slept late.

They do it differently in London.

I woke the next morning at eight, to the prospect of a

lovely, lazy morning with nothing to do but pack a suitcase before the arrival of the final interviewer at noon. I was having breakfast when Leo phoned to read me the *Times* review, which was wonderful. Then Ena got on the line and I asked her to come over and spend the morning with me and she said she was on her way.

A few minutes later, Abbe phoned.

"I thought I'd pick up the four morning papers and bring them to the hotel," she said. And I said:

"Rush right over. Ena's coming and the coffee's hot."

Ena and Abbe arrived together. We spread out the four reviews and read aloud to each other the small headlines proclaiming the show a hit. That was as far as we got when the desk phoned to say Mr. and Mrs. Redington were on the way up. Two minutes later, the desk rang again to say Mr. and Mrs. David Swift were on their way up. Then it was Mr. Roose-Evans, then it was an executive from Futura and a wandering, unscheduled reporter, and after that I lost track.

I phoned Room Service and ordered coffee for ten, and a porter arrived with a banquet urn and ten cups and saucers. But so many people kept on coming that Ena and Abbe had to run back and forth from the living room to the dressing-room sinks, to wash out cups for fresh arrivals at the reception nobody'd told me I was giving.

Some of the guests brought gifts — beautiful scarves that would go in the suitcase and beautiful books that wouldn't — and the Futura executive brought a gift I mean to take with me when I die, on the King Tut theory that you don't know what provisions will be available at the other end. It was a bottle of gin with the only genuine Private Label I ever saw. The printed label read:

GORDON'S
Special Dry
84, Charing Cross Road London
GIN
Distilled by Futura Publications
for
Helene Hanff
to celebrate the opening of
"84, Charing Cross Road"
at the Ambassadors Theatre
26th November, 1981

The last of the guests departed only when and because the final interviewer arrived. He was still there when Sheila came with the car to take me to the airport.

It was December when I got home and through a hectic week of Christmas shopping the dream trip faded a little. Then one morning a thick envelope arrived in the mail from Sue Hyman, enclosing the afternoon reviews. One of them described my walk through the bookshop door to join the cast on stage and added:

"The audience rose to her."

I hadn't seen that, in the blackness beyond the footlights.

I stared at the line till I couldn't see it for tears. Somehow, with that image, the dream week I'd lived through was suddenly, overwhelmingly real. The suite and the flowers and messages were real, the Opening Night was real, even the wildly improbable plaque on a London wall was real. Remembering the desolate evening when I'd learned of Frank Doel's death — when I'd been a failed writer with little to show for her past and no foreseeable future — I was in tears at how that life had been transformed in a single decade.

What fortune teller would ever have had the nerve to predict that the best years of my life would turn out to be my old age?

III "IT WON'T TRAVEL"

That winter and spring, everybody asked me whether the show was coming to Broadway. I answered by quoting a remark André once made, back in the early Seventies when he first came to breakfast.

I'd just read Judith Viorst's *How to Be Hip over Thirty*. I was certain André would publish it if he read it, and when I set the breakfast table I put the book above his plate.

André arrived and stood in the kitchen doorway telling me an anecdote while I put the bacon and eggs on a platter. He was still telling the story as we moved toward the table. As we reached it he broke off in mid-sentence, pointed to the book, said: "I read that, darling, it won't travel," and went on with the story.

From where I'd sat in the Ambassadors Theatre, *84, Charing Cross Road* wouldn't travel. It was more than enough for me that the play was a hit in London. Thanks to James Roose-Evans I spent the winter and spring happily replacing my ragged drapes, my worn-out wall-to-wall carpet and a sofabed that was leaking powdered foam rubber. But late in the summer Alexander H. Cohen bought *84, Charing Cross Road* for Broadway. He'd been a Broadway producer for forty years and I did not drop him a note telling him he was making a mistake.

In September, he phoned to tell me he'd signed Ellen Burstyn to play me and that the show was set to open on the first Tuesday in December. In October a mild interview epidemic began. In November Sheila and Mary Doel wrote to say they were coming to New York for the Opening (leaving their husbands behind as baby-sitters) and Alex Cohen with typical generosity offered to put them up at the Plaza for a week. My oldest friend, Maxine-the-actress, phoned from Hollywood to say she and her husband were coming in for the Opening, since she was a member of the cast of characters.

I went through those months feeling a slowly mounting excitement — and a peaceful sense of detachment. I knew that if a play of mine were about to open on Broadway, I'd be tense and hysterical by turns. But this was James's play. True, it was based on a book I'd written; but the verdict on the book was long in. Or, as I put it to myself placidly:

"It's James's rap."

On the Friday evening before the Opening, I gave a supper party for Sheila and Mary Doel at which everybody (including the hostess) was riding the crest of pre-Opening excitement, heightened by the fact that we had all heard glowing reports from friends who had seen preview performances of *84* and had declared it was bound to be the hit of the season.

On Sunday afternoon, I went to a concert, a cocktail party and then on to dinner. I came home at ten p.m. to find the apartment filled with plants, flowers and telegrams which Dimitria, my excited neighbor across the hall, had taken in for me. The flower arrangements and plants were beautiful and they touched and gratified me, and in a one-room apartment there wasn't any place to put them. While I was distributing them around on tables and windowsills, with a few parked temporarily in the bathtub, the phone rang steadily. Out-of-town friends called to wish me luck;

out-of-town fans called to say they were, or wished they were, here for the Opening.

On Monday, I was out for the evening and when I came home, there were more flowers and plants Dimitria had deposited on the sofa for lack of more suitable space. Since my sofa is also my bed, I was carrying two lovely flower arrangements to the kitchen when — at midnight — the phone rang. A couple from Chicago, ardent fans who had come in for the Opening, were at the other end.

"We know we didn't wake you," the husband said. "We've been trying you all evening."

As I undressed I thought bleakly: "I'll have to get an answering machine." I hate answering machines, I love talking to fans when they call. But not if they were going to start calling at midnight.

On Tuesday evening, I walked to the theatre surrounded by family and closest friends. And the sight of my name on the Nederlander Theatre marquee brought a wave of memories of the noisy melodrama Maxine and I had lived through trying to crash the theatre.

I took my seat in a back row and as the houselights dimmed I reminded myself again complacently:

"It's James's rap."

It was my rap.

I'd accepted congratulations for the words I'd written when they'd moved a London audience to tears; I had to accept responsibility for the same words when they fell with the dull thud of a flop in a Broadway theatre. My family and friends filled too many rows of seats that night. As the evening wore on, I began to feel acutely embarrassed at having lured them all there. I wanted to cut and run so I wouldn't have to face them afterward.

The final curtain fell to perfunctory applause and the

briefest of curtain calls, and I bolted out to the lobby. But everyone who came to say hello to me there seemed in good spirits. So were all the friends who went to Sardi's with me afterward, for the usual party. The party went on till one a.m. — when somebody brought us the first edition of the *Times* with a devastating review of the play.

We picked up the other morning newspapers on the way home and the reviews weren't much kinder. It was after two when I crawled into bed (having first had to dispose of a new batch of flowers and plants) and I was too tired to know what I felt.

But as I opened my eyes the next morning, a thought dropped gently into my mind:

"Thank God it flopped. I couldn't live like this."

I sat bolt upright in shock.

"What kind of a thought was that!" I demanded aloud.

I got up and lit a cigarette and then sat on the edge of the bed and tried to make sense of myself. It wasn't hard to do.

Being a celebrity for a week in London had been the most fun I'd ever had in my life, and wonderful for the ego — but only because I'd known I was coming home at the end of it, home to the quiet, orderly, solitary, unglamorous life I was made for. To be forced to live a celebrity's life at home, even for a little while, had been a nightmarish possibility. It was gone in the morning, like any other nightmare.

"Peace," I said to the understanding room. "Peace."

Q.E.D.

THE BROADWAY PRODUCTION closed after three months, but James's play kept right on going. First there were summer theatre tours, here and in England. Then I began to get letters from actresses playing me in Bath and Edinburgh and Winnipeg — and phone calls from "Helenes" in amateur productions of the play in New Jersey and Delaware and Oregon. Fans sent me programs from productions in Houston, Ontario and Melbourne and a flock of far-off towns I'd never heard of. Not forgetting the American Beauty roses that arrived from the young players in a production at Sierra College in Rocklin, California, or the bowl of dried flowers airmailed to me by an actress named Liz Caiacob who was playing me in Perth, West Australia.

It was — and is — the best of both worlds: the peaceful life of a nobody, with enough fan mail, gifts and phone calls to assure me I'm really somebody. It ought to keep me in a permanent state of gratitude and contentment, and most of the time it does.

But there came an evening last winter when I was curled up in the armchair, too depressed to read. A new book I'd been working on for a year was getting worse instead of better. I wanted to abandon it, but the material in it was all I had to write about. I wondered, if I abandoned it, whether I'd ever write another book.

I thought of *84,* the miracle of my life I would never understand. I thought of *The Duchess,* the trips to London, the dazzling moments that had happened to me there. And like a resentful child when the party's over, I thought:

"What you have got to show for it all?"

I looked around the room. The Futura gin bottle (carefully preserved under a bell jar) stood on a breakfront shelf. The leather-bound *84* was up on a bookshelf. A framed photograph of the plaque hung on an alcove wall. In a long storage cabinet, installed under the bookshelves a few years ago, was a videotape of the TV show alongside a large manila envelope full of brochures from the literary tour and the lovely drawings Ena had made for me of Mama Deutsch's flat and Jane Austen's house. On the bottom shelf of the cabinet were the London reviews.

"Trinkets," I thought sourly, "and yellowing paper."

Then I remembered the sign that had once hung outside Marks & Co.'s bookshop and now occupied the side alcove wall. That, at least, was real. I couldn't see it from where I sat, and I got up, flipped on the alcove light and stepped back a little into the living room to get a good view of it. And then I stood still, rooted — and stared. Not at the sign. At the rows of books that stretched along the back alcove wall.

Except for the few the Queen's bookbinder had restored, they were shabby, faded and discolored. Some had cracked spines, some had covers detached, eaten away by heat and dust. Almost all of them were in some way ravaged by years and use. Like their owner.

"You don't even read them anymore!" I protested silently. "How many do you take down in a year? Five? Six?"

It didn't matter. I had so much of them inside my head they were part of me now. And I was shaken by what I suddenly knew:

If I live to be very old, all my memories of the glory days will grow vague and confused, till I won't be certain any of it really happened. But the books will be there, on my shelves and in my head — the one enduring reality I can be certain of till the day I die.

Of all the gifts in Q's legacy, the first still mattered most and would matter longest. If it took me a lifetime to learn that, Q won't mind. He knows I was never a very bright pupil.